COMPLETE BOOK OF
Grade 2

AMERICAN
EDUCATION
PUBLISHING™

An imprint of Carson-Dellosa Publishing LLC
Greensboro, North Carolina

American Education Publishing™
An imprint of Carson-Dellosa Publishing LLC
P.O. Box 35665
Greensboro, NC 27425 USA

ISBN 0-7696-8582-X
Printed in the USA

06-338127897

Dear Parents, Caregivers, and Educators,

The *Complete Book* series provides young learners an exciting and dynamic way to learn the basic skills essential to learning success. This vivid workbook will guide your student step-by-step through a variety of engaging and developmentally appropriate activities in phonics, reading comprehension, math, problem solving, and writing.

The *Complete Book of Grade 2* is designed for learning reinforcement and can be used as a tool for independent study. This workbook includes:

- High-interest lessons.
- Easy-to-understand examples and directions.
- Challenging concepts presented in simple language.
- Review lessons to measure progress and reinforce skills.
- Expanded teaching suggestions to guide further learning.

To find other learning materials that will interest your young learner and encourage school success, visit www.carsondellosa.com

4

Table of Contents

Reading

All About Me!

Directions: Fill in the blanks to tell all about you!

Name _____
                    (First)   (Last)

Address _____

City _____ State _____

Phone number _____

Age_____

Places I have visited: _____

_____

_____

_____

_____

My favorite hobbies: _____

_____

_____

_____

_____

Let's Begin: b, c, d, f, g, h, j

Directions: Fill in the beginning consonant for each word.

Example: __c__ at

__B__ ox

__J__ acket

__G__ oat

__H__ ouse

__D__ og

__F__ ire

Let's Begin: k, l, m, n, p, q, r

Directions: Write the letter that makes the beginning sound for each picture.

Mouse

_____

rabbit

Nurse

Monkey

lamp

King

rAKC

Queen

pencil

nail

M

Let's Begin: s, t, v, w, x, y, z

Directions: Write the letter under each picture that makes the beginning sound.

ZEbra

SUN

X RAY

VIOLIN

yoyo

WAGON

tent

Last Letters: b, d, f, g

Directions: Fill in the ending consonant for each word.

ma d _____

cu g _____

roo s _____

do g _____

be d _____

bi d _____

Last Letters: k, l, m, n, p, r

Directions: Fill in the ending consonant for each word.

nai _L_____

ca _p_____

gu _m_____

ca _r_____

truc _k_____

ca _p_____

pai _n_____

Last Letters: s, t, x

Directions: Fill in the ending consonant for each word.

ca<u>t</u>_____

bo<u>x</u>_____

bu<u>s</u>_____

fo<u>x</u>_____

boa<u>t</u>_____

ma<u>t</u>_____

Bring on the Blends!

Consonant blends are two or three consonant letters in a word whose sounds combine, or blend. **Examples: br, fr, gr, pr, tr**

Directions: Look at each picture. Say its name. Write the blend you hear at the beginning of each word.

Tree

frag

broom

piesent

Truck

GRAPe
gresp

FRisbe

grass

prum

Triangul

_____

_____

Blends: fl, br, pl, sk, sn

Blends are two consonants put together to form a single sound.

Directions: Look at the pictures and say their names. Write the letters for the beginning sound in each word.

brum

sk

fly

plant

flower

snoon

brush

_____

sner

fly

Blends: bl, sl, cr, cl

Directions: Look at the pictures and say their names. Write the letters for the beginning sound in each word.

_cl_ own   _bl_ anket   _cr_ ayon

_cl_ ock   _sl_ ide   _cl_ oud

_cl_ ed   _cr_ ab   _cr_ ocodile

Tell Me a Riddle

Directions: Write a word from the word box to answer each riddle.

clock	blow	climb	slipper
gloves	clap	blocks	flashlight

1. You need me when the lights go out.
   What am I? _flashlight_

2. People use me to tell the time.
   What am I? _clock_

3. You put me on your hands in the winter to keep them warm.
   What am I? _gloves_

4. Cinderella lost one like me at midnight.
   What am I? _slipper_

5. This is what you do with your hands when you are pleased.
   What is it? _clap_

6. You can do this with a whistle or with bubble gum.
   What is it? _blow_

7. These are what you might use to build a castle when you are playing.
   What are they? _blocks_

8. You do this to get to the top of a hill.
   What is it? _climb_

Teammates

Consonant teams are two or three consonant letters that have a single sound. **Examples: sh** and **tch**

Directions: Write each word from the word box next to its picture. Underline the consonant team in each word. Circle the consonant team in each word in the box.

bench	match	shoe	thimble	shell
peach	watch	whale	chair	wheel

shoe

match

wheel

watch

chair

peach

whale

bench

thimble

shell

Join the Team

Directions: Look at the first picture in each row. Circle the pictures that have the same sound.

whistle

shoe

chin

thumb

Sort It Out

Directions: Look at the words in the word box. Write all of the words that end with the **ng** sound in the column under the picture of the **ring**. Write all of the words that end with the **nk** sound under the picture of the **sink**. Finish the sentences with words from the word box.

strong	rank	bring	bank	honk	hang	thank
long	hunk	song	stung	bunk	sang	junk

ng

strong

long

song

sang

hang

bring

stung

nk

rank

hunk

bank

honk

thank

jonk

bunk

1. _____ your horn when you get to my house.

2. He was _____ by a bumblebee.

3. We are going to put our money in a ___bank___.

4. I want to ___bring___ you for the birthday present.

5. My brother and I sleep in ___bunk___ beds.

Shhh! Silent Letters

Some words have letters you can't hear at all, such as the **gh** in **night**, the **w** in **wrong**, the **l** in **walk**, the **k** in **knee**, the **b** in **climb** and the **t** in **listen**.

Directions: Look at the words in the word box. Write the word under its picture. Underline the silent letters.

knife	light	calf	wrench	lamb	eight
wrist	whistle	comb	thumb	knob	knee

eight

wrist

knee

calf

comb

lamb

wistle

light

wrench

knob

thumb

knife

Review

Directions: Read the story. Circle the consonant teams (two or three letters) and silent letters in the underlined words. Be sure to check for more than one team in a word! One has been done for you.

One day last (Spring) my family went on a (picnic). My father (picked) out a pretty spot next to a (stream). While my (brother) and I (climbed) a (tree), my mother (spread) out a (sheet) and (placed) the food on it. But before we could eat, a (skunk) (walked) out of the woods! Mother (screamed) and scared the skunk. It (sprayed) us with a terrible smell! Now, we think it is a funny story. But that day, we ran!

Directions: Write the words with three-letter blends on the lines.

_____

_____

_____

_____

Double Duty: Hard and Soft c

When **c** is followed by **e**, **i** or **y**, it usually has a **soft** sound. The **soft c** sounds like **s**. For example, **c**ircle and fen**c**e. When **c** is followed by **a** or **u**, it usually has a **hard** sound. The **hard c** sounds like **k**. For example, **c**up and **c**art.

Directions: Read the words in the word box. Write the words in the correct lists. One word will be in both. Write a word from the box to finish each sentence.

| pencil | cookie | dance | popcorn | cent |
| circus | lucky | mice | tractor | card |

Words with soft c   **Words with hard c**

__pencil__   _Tractor_

_____   _____

_____   _____

_____   _____

_____   _____

_____   _____

                 _____

1. Another word for a penny is a _____.

2. A cat likes to chase _____.

3. You will see animals and clowns at

   the _____.

4. Will you please sharpen my _____?

Double Duty: Hard and Soft g

When **g** is followed by **e**, **i** or **y**, it usually has a **soft** sound. The **soft g** sounds like **j**. **Example:** change and gentle. The **hard g** sounds like the **g** in girl or gate.

Directions: Read the words in the word box. Write the words in the correct lists. Write a word from the box to finish each sentence.

engine	glove	cage
magic	frog	giant
flag	large	glass
goose		

Words with soft g	**Words with hard g**
engine	_____
_____	_____
_____	_____
_____	_____
_____	_____

1. Our bird lives in a _____.

2. Pulling a rabbit from a hat is a good

   _____ trick.

3. A car needs an _____ to run.

4. A _____ is a huge person.

5. An elephant is a very _____ animal.

Letter Detector: Short Vowels

Vowels can make **short** or **long** sounds. The **short a** sounds like the **a** in c**a**t. The **short e** is like the **e** in l**e**g. The **short i** sounds like the **i** in p**i**g. The **short o** sounds like the **o** in b**o**x. The **short u** sounds like the **u** in c**u**p.

Directions: Look at each picture. Write the missing short vowel letter.

p _u_ p   n _e_ t   s _o_ ck

_a_ x   l _i_ ps   h _a_ t

f _o_ x   t _e_ nt   p _i_ n

Super Silent e

Long vowel sounds have the same sound as their names. When a **Super Silent e** appears at the end of a word, you can't hear it, but it makes the other vowel have a long sound. For example: **tub** has a **short** vowel sound, and **tube** has a **long** vowel sound.

Directions: Look at the following pictures. Decide if the word has a short or long vowel sound. Circle the correct word. Watch for the **Super Silent e**!

can (cane)　(tub) tube　rob (robe)

(pin) pine　(cap) cape　not (note)

slid (slide)　dim (dime)　tap (tape)

Letter Detector: Long Vowels

Directions: Say the name of the pictures. Listen for the long vowel sounds. Write the missing long vowel sound under each picture.

c a ke   h i ke   n o se

a pe   c u be   gr a pe

r a ke   b o ne   k i te

Review

Directions: Read the words in each box. Cross out the word that does not belong.

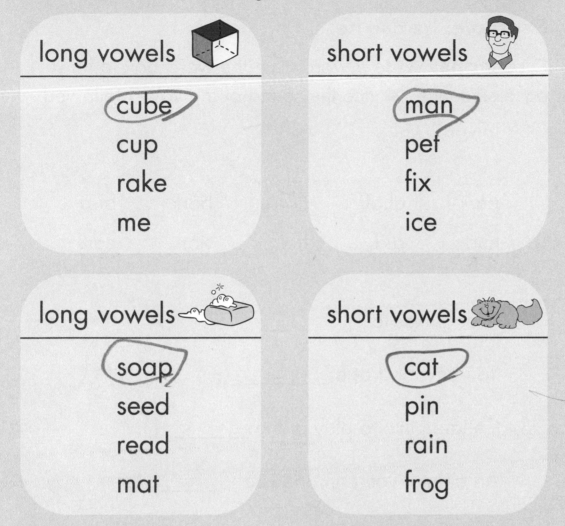

long vowels

~~cube~~
cup
rake
me

short vowels

~~man~~
pet
fix
ice

long vowels

~~soap~~
seed
read
mat

short vowels

~~cat~~
pin
rain
frog

Directions: Write **short** or **long** to label the words in each box.

_____ vowels

~~hose~~
take
bead
cube
eat
see

_____ vowels

hose
take
bead
cube
eat
see

R in Charge

When a vowel is followed by the letter **r**, it has a different sound.

Example: he and **her**

Directions: Write a word from the word box to finish each sentence. Notice the sound of the vowel followed by an **r**.

park　chair　horse　bark　bird
hurt　girl　hair　store　ears

1. A dog likes to _bark_.

2. You buy food at a _store_.

3. Children like to play at the _park_.

4. An animal you can ride is a _____.

5. You hear with your _horse_.

6. A robin is a kind of _brid_.

7. If you fall down, you might get _ears_.

8. The opposite of a boy is a _girl_.

9. You comb and brush your _hair_.

10. You sit down on a _chare_.

Double Trouble

Usually when two vowels appear together, the first one says its name and the second one is silent.

Example: bean

Directions: Unscramble the double vowel words below. Write the correct word on the line.

ocat _coat_

mtea _meat_

teas _seats_

ogat _goat_

atli _tail_

etar _tear_

eetf _feet_

otab _boat_

spea _peas_

apil _pail_

Team Time: ou, ow, au, aw

The vowel teams **ou** and **ow** can have the same sound. You can hear it in the words **clown** and **cloud**. The vowel teams **au** and **aw** have the same sound. You hear it in the words **because** and **law**.

Directions: Look at the pictures. Write the correct vowel team to complete the words. The first one is done for you. You may need to use a dictionary to help you with the correct spelling.

__au__ to   cl_ow_n   h_ou_se

fl_ow_er   s_aw_   _ow_l

p_ow_der   m_ow_th   j_aw_

Team Time: ea

The vowel team **ea** can have a **short e** sound like in **head**, or a **long e** sound like in **bead**. An **ea** followed by an **r** makes a sound like the one in **ear** or like the one in **heard**.

Directions: Read the story. Listen for the sound **ea** makes in the bold words.

Have you ever **read** a book or **heard** a story about a **bear**? You might have **learned** that bears sleep through the winter. Some bears may sleep the whole **season**. Sometimes they look almost **dead**! But they are very much alive. As the cold winter passes and the spring **weather** comes **near**, they wake up. After such a nice rest, they must be **ready** to **eat** a **really** big **meal**!

words with long ea

_____

_____

_____

_____

words with short ea   **ea followed by r**

_____   _____

_____   _____

_____   _____

_____   _____

Team Time: ie, ei, eigh, ey

The vowel team **ie** makes the **long e** sound like in **believe**. The team **ei** also makes the **long e** sound like in **either**. But **ei** can also make a **long a** sound like in **eight**.

Directions: Circle the **ei** words with the **long a** sound.

neighbor   veil   receive

reindeer   reign   ceiling

The teams **eigh** and **ey** also make the **long a** sound.

Directions: Finish the sentences with words from the word box.

obey   weigh   thief   field   ceiling

1. Rules are for us to _____.

2. The bird got out of its cage and flew up to the

   _____.

3. How much do you _____?

4. They caught the _____ who took my bike.

5. Corn grows in a _____.

Team Time: oi, oy, ou, ow

Directions: Look at the first picture in each row. Circle the pictures that have the same sound.

oil

toy

couch

howl

Team Time: ai, ee

Directions: Write in the vowel team **ai** or **ee** to complete each word.

r_____n

f_____d

s_____d

p_____l

s_____l

cr_____k

Review

Directions: Read the story. Fill in the blanks with words from the word box.

| cookies | Joe | bowl | tooth | flour | eight |
| spoon | eats | enjoys | round | boy | either |

Do you like to cook? I know a _____

named _____ who loves to cook. When

Joe has a sweet _____, he makes

_____. He puts _____

and sugar in a _____ and stirs it with a

_____. Then, he adds the butter and

eggs. He makes cookies that are _____

or other shapes. He likes them _____

way. Now is the part he _____ the

most: Joe _____ the cookies. He might

eat seven or _____ at a time!

That's Y!

When **y** comes at the end of a word, it is a vowel. When **y** is the only vowel at the end of a one-syllable word, it has the sound of a **long i** (like in **my**). When **y** is the only vowel at the end of a word with more than one syllable, it has the sound of a **long e** (like in **baby**).

Directions: Look at the words in the word box. If the word has the sound of a **long i**, write it under the word **my**. If the word has the sound of a **long e**, write it under the word **baby**. Write the word from the word box that answers each riddle.

| happy | penny | fry | try | dry |
| bunny | windy | sky | party | fly |

my   **baby**

my	baby
fry	penny
dry	windy
fly	happy
fry	bunny
sky	party

1. It takes five of these to make a nickel. _penny_

2. This is what you call a baby rabbit. _bunny_

3. It is often blue and you can see it if you look up. _____

4. You might have one of these on your birthday. _party_

Putting It Together

Compound words are two words that are put together to make one new word.

Directions: Read the sentences. Fill in the blank with a compound word from the box.

> raincoat bedroom lunchbox hallway sandbox

1. A box with sand is a

   sandbox.

2. The way through a hall is a

   hallway.

3. A box for lunch is a

   lunchbox.

4. A coat for the rain is a

   raincoat.

5. A room with a bed is a

   bedroom.

What's Cooking?

Compound words are formed by putting together two smaller words.

Directions: Help the cook brew her stew. Mix words from the first column with words from the second column to make new words. Write your new words on the lines at the bottom.

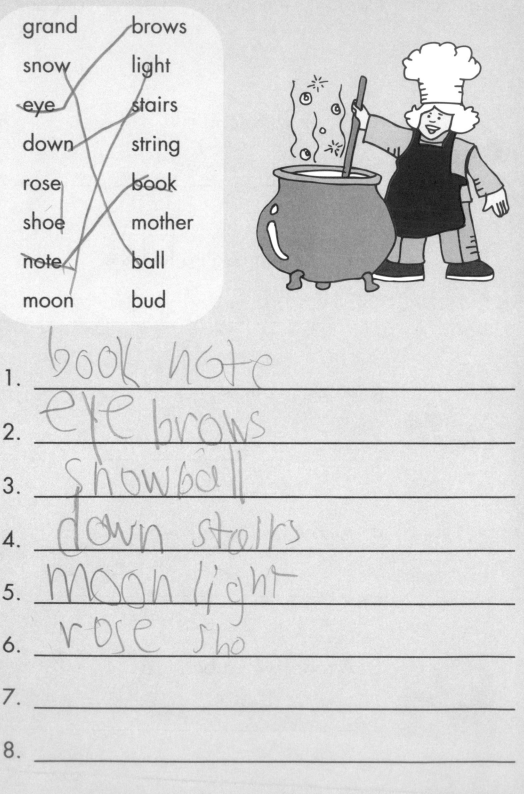

grand	brows
snow	light
eye	stairs
down	string
rose	book
shoe	mother
note	ball
moon	bud

1. book note

2. eye brows

3. snowball

4. down stairs

5. moon light

6. rose sho

7. _____

8. _____

Two-for-One Special

Directions: Draw a line under the compound word in each sentence. On the line, write the two words that make up the compound word.

1. A firetruck came to help put out the fire.

_____

2. I will be nine years old on my next birthday.

_____

3. We built a treehouse at the back.

_____

4. Dad put a scarecrow in his garden.

_____

5. It is fun to make footprints in the snow.

_____

6. I like to read the comics in the newspaper.

_____

7. Cowboys ride horses and use lassos.

_____

Short and Sweet

Contractions are a short way to write two words, such as **isn't**, **I've** and **weren't**. **Example: it is = it's**

Directions: Draw a line from each word pair to its contraction.

I am	she's
it is	they're
you are	we're
we are	he's
they are	I'm
she is	it's
he is	you're

We Love Contractions!

Directions: Cut out the two words and put them together to show what two words make the contraction. Glue them over the contraction.

- -

cut out

This page is blank for the cutting activity
on the opposite side.

Put Your Hands Together

Words are made up of parts called **syllables**. Each syllable has a vowel sound. One way to count syllables is to clap as you say the word.

Example:
cat	1 clap	1 syllable
table	2 claps	2 syllables
butterfly	3 claps	3 syllables

Directions: "Clap out" the words below. Write how many syllables each word has.

movie _____

piano _____

tree _____

bicycle _____

sun _____

cabinet _____

football _____

dog _____

basket _____

swimmer _____

rainbow _____

paper _____

picture _____

Give Me a Break

Dividing a word into syllables can help you read a new word. You also might divide syllables when you are writing if you run out of space on a line. Many words contain two consonants that are next to each other. A word can usually be divided between two consonants.

Directions: Divide each word into two syllables. The first one is done for you.

kitten   _____ kit   ten _____

lumber   _____

batter   _____

winter   _____

funny   _____

harder   _____

dirty   _____

sister   _____

Break it Up!

When a double consonant is used in the middle of a word, the word can usually be divided between the consonants.

Directions: Look at the words in the word box. Divide each word into two syllables. Leave space between each syllable. One is done for you.

butter	puppy	kitten	yellow
dinner	chatter	ladder	happy
pillow	letter	mitten	summer

<u>but</u> <u>ter</u>   _____   _____

_____   _____   _____

_____   _____   _____

_____   _____   _____

Many words are divided between two consonants that are not alike.

Directions: Look at the words in the word box. Divide each word into two syllables. One is done for you.

window	doctor	number
mister	winter	pencil
barber	sister	picture

<u>win</u> <u>dow</u>   _____   _____

_____   _____   _____

_____   _____   _____

Add It On

A **suffix** is a syllable that is added at the end of a word to change its meaning.

Directions: Add the suffixes to the root words to make new words. Use your new words to complete the sentences.

help + ful = _____

care + less = _____

talk + ed = _____

love + ly = _____

loud + er = _____

1. My mother _____ to my teacher about my homework.

2. The radio was _____ than the television.

3. Sally is always _____ to her mother.

4. The flowers are _____.

5. It is _____ to cross the street without looking both ways.

Backward Nan

Directions: Read the story. Underline the words that end with **est**, **ed** or **ing**. On the lines below, write the root words for each word you underlined.

The funniest book I ever read was about a girl named Nan. Nan did everything backward. She even spelled her name backward. Nan slept in the day and played at night. She dried her hair before washing it. She turned on the light after she finished her book—which she read from the back to the front! When it rained, Nan waited until she was inside before opening her umbrella. She even walked backward. The silliest part: The only thing Nan did forward was back up!

1. _____   8. _____

2. _____   9. _____

3. _____   10. _____

4. _____   11. _____

5. _____   12. _____

6. _____   13. _____

7. _____

The Three Rs

Prefixes are syllables added to the beginning of words that change their meaning. The prefix **re** means "again."

Directions: Read the story. Then, follow the instructions.

Kim wants to find ways she can save the Earth. She studies the "three R's"—reduce, reuse and recycle. Reduce means to make less. Both reuse and recycle mean to use again.

Add **re** to the beginning of each word below. Use the new words to complete the sentences.

_____ build _____ fill

_____ read _____ tell

_____ write _____ run

1. The race was a tie, so Dawn and Kathy had to

   _____ it.

2. The block wall fell down, so Simon had to

   _____ it.

3. The water bottle was empty, so Luna had to

   _____ it.

4. Javier wrote a good story, but he wanted to

   _____ it to make it better.

5. The teacher told a story, and students had to

   _____ it.

6. Toni didn't understand the directions, so she had to

   _____ them.

Prefix Power

Directions: Change the meaning of the sentences by adding the prefixes to the **bold** words.

The boy was **lucky** because he guessed the answer **correctly**.

The boy was (un) _____ because he

guessed the answer (in) _____ .

When Mary **behaved**, she felt **happy**.

When Mary (mis) _____ ,

she felt (un) _____ .

Mike wore his jacket **buttoned** because the dance was **formal**.

Mike wore his jacket (un) _____

because the dance was (in) _____ .

Tim **understood** because he was **familiar** with the book.

Tim (mis) _____ because he was

(un) _____ with the book.

Review

Directions: Read each sentence. Look at the words in **bold**. Circle the prefix and write the root word on the line.

1. The **preview** of the movie was funny.

   _____

2. We always drink **nonfat** milk.

   _____

3. We will have to **reschedule** the trip.

   _____

4. Are you tired of **reruns** on television?

   _____

5. I have **outgrown** my new shoes already.

   _____

6. You must have **misplaced** the papers.

   _____

7. Police **enforce** the laws of the city.

   _____

8. I **disliked** that book.

   _____

9. The boy **distrusted** the big dog.

   _____

10. Try to **enjoy** yourself at the party.

   _____

Mike's Bike

Directions: Read the story about bike safety. Answer the questions below the story.

Mike has a red bike. He likes his bike. Mike wears a helmet. Mike wears knee pads and elbow pads. They keep him safe. Mike stops at signs. Mike looks both ways. Mike is safe on his bike.

1. What color is Mike's bike? ___red___

2. Which sentence in the story tells why Mike wears pads and a helmet? Write it here.

   ___to not hrut his head and knees___

3. What else does Mike do to keep safe?

   He ___stops___ at signs and ___looks___ both ways.

Total Recall

Directions: Read about Nikki's pets. Then, answer the questions.

Nikki has two cats, Tiger and Sniffer, and two dogs, Spot and Wiggles. Tiger is an orange striped cat who likes to sleep under a big tree and pretend she is a real tiger. Sniffer is a gray cat who likes to sniff the flowers in Nikki's garden. Spot is a Dalmatian with many black spots. Wiggles is a big furry brown dog who wiggles all over when he is happy.

1. Which dog is brown and furry? _Wiggles_

2. What color is Tiger? _orange_

3. What kind of dog is Spot? _a dallmason_

4. Which cat likes to sniff flowers? _Nikki's_

5. Where does Tiger like to sleep? _a tree_

_____

6. Who wiggles all over when he is happy?

Wiggles

Nikki's Garden

People on the Go

Directions: Read the story about different kinds of transportation. Answer the questions with words from the story.

People use many kinds of transportation. Boats float on the water. Some people fish in a boat. Airplanes fly in the sky. Flying in a plane is a fast way to get somewhere. Trains run on a track. The first car is the engine. The last car is the caboose. Some people even sleep in beds on a train! A car has four wheels. Most people have a car. A car rides on roads. A bus can hold many people. A bus rides on roads. Most children ride a bus to school.

1. A boat floats on the __water__.

2. If you want to get somewhere fast, which transportation would you use?

   _____

3. The first car on a train is called an engine and the

   last car is a _____.

4. _____ ride on a bus.

5. A _____ has four wheels.

Dairy Delights

Directions: Read the story. Answer the questions. Try the recipe.

Cows Give Us Milk

Cows live on a farm. The farmer milks the cows to get the milk. Many things are made from milk. We make ice cream, sour cream, cottage cheese and butter from milk. Butter is fun to make! You can learn to make your own butter. First, you need cream. Put the cream in a jar and shake it. Then, you need to pour off the liquid. Next, you put the butter in a bowl. Add a little salt and stir! Finally, spread it on crackers and eat!

1. What animal gives us milk?_____

2. What 4 things are made from milk?

   _____   _____

   _____   _____

3. What did the story teach you to make?_____

4. Put the steps in order. Place 1, 2, 3, 4 by the sentence.

   _____ Spread the butter on crackers and eat!

   _____ Shake cream in a jar.

   _____ Start with cream.

   _____ Add salt to the butter.

Get the Story Straight

Spencer likes to make new friends. Today, he made friends with the dog in the picture.

Directions: Number the sentences in order to find out what Spencer did today.

_____ Spencer kissed his mother good-bye.

_____ Spencer saw the new dog next door.

_____ Spencer went outside.

_____ Spencer said hello.

_____ Spencer got dressed and ate breakfast.

_____ Spencer woke up.

Snacktime!

Alana and Marcus are hungry for a snack. They want to make nacho chips and cheese. The steps they need to follow are all mixed up.

Directions: Read the steps. Number them in 1, 2, 3 order. Then, color the picture.

_____ Bake the chips in the oven for 2 minutes.

_____ Get a cookie sheet to bake on.

_____ Get out the nacho chips and cheese.

_____ Eat the nachos and chips.

_____ Put the chips on the cookie sheet.

_____ Put grated cheese on the chips.

Rain, Rain, Go Away

Directions: Read about rain. Then, follow the instructions.

Clouds are made up of little drops of ice and water. They push and bang into each other. Then, they join together to make bigger drops and begin to fall. More raindrops cling to them. They become heavy and fall quickly to the ground.

Write **first**, **second**, **third**, **fourth** and **fifth** to put the events in order.

_____ More raindrops cling to them.

_____ Clouds are made up of little drops of ice and water.

_____ They join together and make bigger drops that begin to fall.

_____ The drops of ice and water bang into each other.

_____ The drops become heavy and fall quickly to the ground.

Follow Me

Directions: Read the sentences. Follow the instructions.

1. On Monday, Lisa needs bread. Use a **red** crayon to mark her path from her house to that building.

   Where does she go? _____

2. On Tuesday, Lisa wants to read books. Use a **green** crayon to mark her path.

   Where does she go? _____

3. On Wednesday, Lisa wants to swing. Use a **yellow** crayon to mark her path.

   Where does she go? _____

4. On Thursday, Lisa wants to buy stamps. Use a **black** crayon to mark her path.

   Where does she go? _____

5. On Friday, Lisa wants to get money. Use a **purple** crayon to mark her path.

   Where does she go? _____

Map It!

Directions: Study the map of the United States. Follow the instructions.

1. Draw a star on the state where you live.

2. Draw a line from your state to the Atlantic Ocean.

3. Draw a triangle in the Gulf of Mexico.

4. Draw a circle in the Pacific Ocean.

5. Color each state that borders your state a different color.

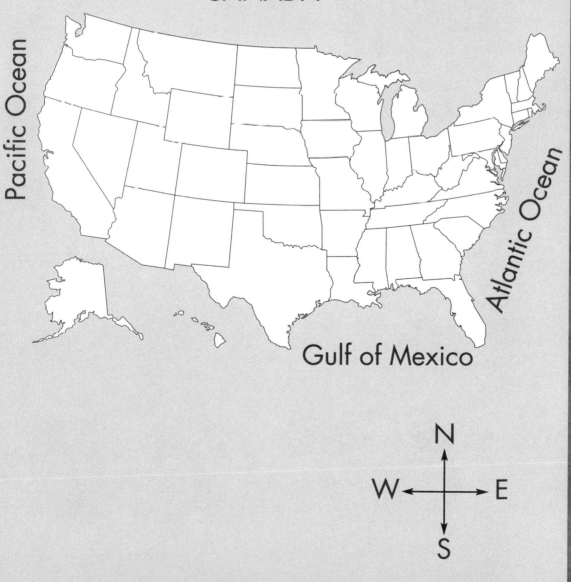

CANADA

Pacific Ocean

Atlantic Ocean

Gulf of Mexico

N
W   E
S

Dare to Be Different

Directions: Look at the pictures. Draw an **X** on the picture in each row that is different.

Birds of a Feather

Directions: Read about parrots and bluebirds. Then, complete the Venn diagram, telling how they are the same and different.

Bluebirds and parrots are both birds. Bluebirds and parrots can fly. They both have beaks. Parrots can live inside a cage. Bluebirds must live outdoors.

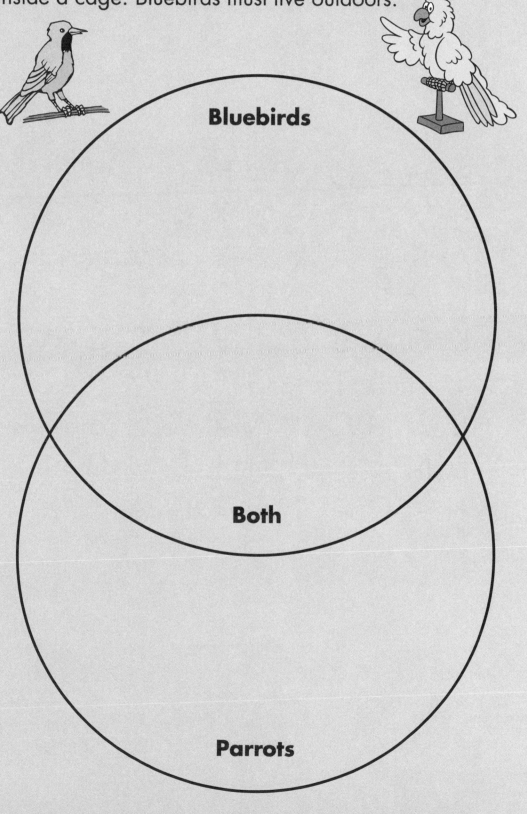

Bluebirds

Both

Parrots

Classifying Critters

Directions: Use a **red** crayon to circle the names of three animals that would make good pets. Use a **blue** crayon to circle the names of three wild animals. Use an **orange** crayon to circle the two animals that live on a farm.

BEAR	CAT	LION	SHEEP
BIRD	DOG	COW	TIGER

```
A M E O W W N L I O N
B M D O G G X I I S O
A B E A R R V L M H R
R M R M O O U S E E K
K C A B B I R D S E M
I O T T I G E R M P Q
B W N O W W R Q N E N
D N C P H H I D U D N
F K C A T T R O A R M
```

Rainy Day Play

Directions: Read the story. Then, circle the objects Jonathan needs to stay dry.

It is raining. Jonathan wants to play outdoors. What should he wear to stay dry? What should he carry to stay dry?

Art Smart

Directions: Read about art tools. Then, color only the art tools.

Andrea uses different art tools to help her design her masterpieces. To cut, she needs scissors. To draw, she needs a pencil. To color, she needs crayons. To paint, she needs a brush.

Write which tools are needed to:

draw   color   cut

_____   _____   _____

Super Groups

Directions: The words in each box form a group. Choose the word from the word box that describes each group and write it on the line.

clothes   family   noises   colors   flowers

fruits   animals   coins   toys

rose
buttercup
tulip
daisy

_____

crash
bang
ring
pop

_____

mother
father
sister
brother

_____

puzzle
wagon
blocks
doll

_____

green
purple
blue
red

_____

grapes
orange
apple
plum

_____

shirt
socks
dress
coat

_____

dime
penny
nickel
quarter

_____

dog
horse
elephant
moose

_____

Tricky Tree

This tricky tree has four different kinds of leaves: ash, poison ivy, silver maple and white oak.

Directions: Follow the instructions. Then, answer the questions.

1. Underline the white oak leaves.

   How many are there? _____

2. Circle the ash leaves.

   How many are there? _____

3. Draw an **X** on the poison ivy leaves.

   How many are there? _____

4. Draw a box around the silver maple leaves.

   How many are there? _____

A Look at Ladybugs

Directions: Read about ladybugs. Then, answer the questions.

Have you ever seen a ladybug? Ladybugs are red. They have black spots. They have six legs. Ladybugs are pretty!

1. What color are ladybugs? _____

2. What color are their spots? _____

3. How many legs do ladybugs have? _____

Paper Puppets

Directions: Read about paper-bag puppets. Then, follow the instructions.

It is easy to make a hand puppet. You need a small paper bag. You need colored paper. You need glue. You need scissors. Are you ready?

1. Circle the main idea:

   You need scissors.

   Making a hand puppet is easy.

2. Write the four objects you need to make a paper-bag puppet.

   1) _____

   2) _____

   3) _____

   4) _____

3. Draw a face on the paper-bag puppet.

Nice to Meet You

Directions: Read about how to meet a dog. Then, follow the instructions.

Do not try to pet a dog right away. First, let the dog sniff your hand. Do not move quickly. Do not talk loudly. Just let the dog sniff.

1. Predict what the dog will let you do if it likes you.

    _____

    _____

2. What should you let the dog do? _____

    _____

3. Name three things you should not do when you meet a dog.

    1) _____

    2) _____

    3) _____

Sean Leads the Team

Directions: Read about Sean's basketball game. Then, answer the questions.

Sean really likes to play basketball. One sunny day, he decided to ask his friends to play basketball at the park, but there were six people—Sean, Aki, Lance, Kate, Zac and Oralia. A basketball team only allows five to play at a time. So, Sean decided to be the coach. Sean and his friends had fun.

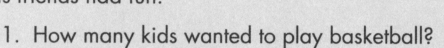

1. How many kids wanted to play basketball? _____

2. Write their names in ABC order:

   _____

   _____

   _____

   _____

   _____

   _____

3. How many players can play on a basketball team

   at a time? _____

4. Where did they play basketball? _____

5. Who decided to be the coach? _____

Rained Out

Predicting is telling what is likely to happen based on the facts.

Directions: Read the story. Then, check each sentence below that tells how the story could end.

One cloudy day, Juan and his baseball team, the Bears, played the Crocodiles. It was the last half of the fifth inning, and it started to rain. The coaches and umpires had to decide what to do.

_____ They kept playing until nine innings were finished.

_____ They ran for cover and waited until the rain stopped.

_____ Each player grabbed an umbrella and returned to the field to finish the game.

_____ They canceled the game and played it another day.

_____ They acted like crocodiles and slid around the wet bases.

_____ The coaches played the game while the players sat in the dugout.

Dog-Gone!

Directions: Read the story. Then, follow the instructions.

Scotty and Simone were washing their dog, Willis. His fur was wet. Their hands were wet. Willis did NOT like to be wet. Scotty dropped the soap. Simone picked it up and let go of Willis. Uh-oh!

1. Write what happened next.

_____

_____

_____

2. Draw what happened next.

Game Time!

A **fact** is something that can be proven. An **opinion** is a feeling or belief about something and cannot be proven.

Directions: Read these sentences about different games. Then, write **F** next to each fact and **O** next to each opinion.

_____ 1. Tennis is cool!

_____ 2. There are red and black markers in a Checkers game.

_____ 3. In football, a touchdown is worth six points.

_____ 4. Being a goalie in soccer is easy.

_____ 5. A yo-yo moves on a string.

_____ 6. June's sister looks like the queen on the card.

_____ 7. The six kids need three more players for a baseball team.

_____ 8. Table tennis is more fun than court tennis.

Owls Are a Hoot

Directions: Read the story. Then, follow the instructions.

My name is Owen Owl, and I am a bird. I go to Nocturnal School. Our teacher is Mr. Screech Owl. In his class I learned that owls are birds and can sleep all day and hunt at night. Some of us live in nests in trees. In North America, it is against the law to harm owls. I like being an owl!

Write **F** next to each fact and **O** next to each opinion.

_____ 1. No one can harm owls in North America.

_____ 2. It would be great if owls could talk.

_____ 3. Owls sleep all day.

_____ 4. Some owls sleep in nests.

_____ 5. Mr. Screech Owl is a good teacher.

_____ 6. Owls are birds.

_____ 7. Owen Owl would be a good friend.

_____ 8. Owls hunt at night.

Chef Jeff

Directions: Read the story. Then, answer the questions.

Jeff is baking cookies. He wears special clothes when he bakes. He puts flour, sugar, eggs and butter into a bowl. He mixes everything together. He puts the cookies in the oven at 11:15 A.M. It takes 15 minutes for the cookies to bake. Jeff wants something cold and white to drink when he eats his cookies.

1. Is Jeff baking a cake?   Yes   No

2. What are two things that Jeff might wear when he bakes?

   hat   boots   apron   tie   raincoat   roller skates

3. What didn't Jeff put in the cookies?

   flour   eggs   milk   butter   sugar

4. What do you think Jeff does after he mixes the cookies but before he bakes them?

   _____

   _____

5. What time will the cookies be done? _____

6. What will Jeff drink with his cookies? _____

7. Why do you think Jeff wanted to bake cookies?

   _____

   _____

Mother's Helper

Directions: Read more about sea horses. Then, answer the questions.

A father sea horse helps the mother. He has a small sack or pouch, on the front of his body. The mother sea horse lays the eggs. She does not keep them. She gives the eggs to the father.

1. What does the mother sea horse do with her eggs?

_____

2. Where does the father sea horse put the eggs?

_____

3. Sea horses can change color. Color the sea horses.

What Do You See?

Directions: Read this story about Ling and Bradley. Draw pictures for the beginning and middle to describe each part of the story.

Beginning: One sunny day, Ling and Bradley, wearing their empty backpacks, rode their bikes down the street to the park.

Middle: They stopped by an oak tree with many acorns under it. They picked up some and stuffed them into their backpacks.

Directions: Draw an ending for this story that tells what you think they did with the acorns.

End: With the heavy backpacks strapped on their backs, they pedaled home.

It's No Problem!

Juniper has three problems to solve. She needs your help.

Directions: Read each problem. Write what you think she should do.

1. Juniper is watching her favorite TV show when the power goes out.

_____

_____

_____

_____

2. Juniper is riding her bike to school when the front tire goes flat.

_____

_____

_____

_____

3. Juniper loses her father while shopping in the supermarket.

_____

_____

_____

_____

Picture This

Directions: Draw three pictures to tell a story about each topic.

1. Feeding a pet

2. Playing with a friend

Beginning

Beginning

Middle

Middle

End

End

Bookworms

Directions: Use the clues to help the children find their books. Draw a line from each child's name to the correct book.

Brett   Aki   Lorenzo   Kate   Zac   Oralia

CHILDREN	BOOKS
Brett	jokes
Aki	cakes
Lorenzo	monsters
Kate	games
Zac	flags
Oralia	space

Clues

1. Lorenzo likes jokes.

2. Kate likes to bake.

3. Oralia likes far away places.

4. Aki does not like monsters or flags.

5. Zac does not like space or monsters.

6. Brett does not like games, jokes or cakes.

What's for Dinner?

Dad is cooking dinner tonight. You can find out what day of the week it is.

Directions: Read the clues. Complete the menu. Answer the question.

Menu

Monday _____

Tuesday _____

Wednesday _____

Thursday _____

Friday_____

Saturday _____

Sunday_____

1. Mom fixed pizza on Monday.

2. Dad fixed cheese rolls the day before that.

3. Tess made meat pie three days after Mom fixed pizza.

4. Tom fixed corn-on-the-cob the day before Tess made meat pie.

5. Mom fixed hot dogs the day after Tess made meat pie.

6. Tess cooked fish the day before Dad fixed cheese rolls.

7. Dad is making chicken today. What day is it?

_____

Review

Directions: Read the story. Then, answer the questions.

Randa, Emily, Ali, Dave, Liesl and Deana all love to read. Every Tuesday, they all go to the library together and pick out their favorite books. Randa likes books about fish. Emily likes books about sports and athletes. Ali likes books about art. Dave likes books about wild animals. Liesl likes books with riddles and puzzles. Deanna likes books about cats and dogs.

1. Circle the main idea:

   Randa, Emily, Ali, Dave, Liesl and Deana are good friends.

   Randa, Emily, Ali, Dave, Liesl and Deana all like books.

2. Who do you think might grow up to be an artist?

   _____

3. Who do you think might grow up to be an oceanographer (someone who studies the ocean)?

   _____

4. Who do you think might grow up to be a veterinarian (an animal doctor)?

   _____

5. Who do you think might grow up to be a zookeeper (someone who cares for zoo animals)?

   _____

Twister Tips

Directions: Read about tornadoes. Then, follow the instructions.

A tornado begins over land with strong winds and thunderstorms. The spinning air becomes a funnel. It can cause damage. If you are inside, go to the lowest floor of the building. A basement is a safe place. A bathroom or closet in the middle of a building can be a safe place, too. If you are outside, lie in a ditch. Remember, tornadoes are dangerous.

Write five facts about tornadoes.

1. _____

_____

2. _____

_____

3. _____

_____

4. _____

_____

5. _____

_____

What a Breeze!

The setting is where a story takes place. The characters are the people in a story or play.

Directions: Read about Hercules. Then, answer the questions.

Hercules was born in the warm Atlantic Ocean. He was a very small and weak baby. He wanted to be the strongest hurricane in the world. But he had one problem. He couldn't blow 75-mile-per-hour winds. Hercules blew and blew in the ocean, until one day, his sister, Hola, told him it would be more fun to be a breeze than a hurricane. Hercules agreed. It was a breeze to be a breeze!

1. What is the setting of the story?

   _____

2. Who are the characters?

   _____

3. What is the problem?

   _____

4. How does Hercules solve his problem?

   _____

   _____

Red, White, and Blue

Directions: Read each story. Then, write whether it is fiction or nonfiction.

One sunny day in July, a dog named Stan ran away from home. He went up one street and down the other looking for fun, but all the yards were empty. Where was everybody? Stan kept walking until he heard the sound of band music and happy people. Stan walked faster until he got to Central Street. There he saw men, women, children and dogs getting ready to walk in a parade. It was the Fourth of July!

Fiction or Nonfiction? _____

Americans celebrate the Fourth of July every year, because it is the birthday of the United States of America. On July 4, 1776, the United States got its independence from Great Britain. Today, Americans celebrate this holiday with parades, picnics and fireworks as they proudly wave the red, white and blue American flag.

Fiction or Nonfiction? _____

Hisssss!

Directions: Write a fictional (make-believe) story about a snake. Make sure to include details and a title.

_____
title

_____

_____

_____

_____

_____

_____

_____

_____

_____

_____

_____

English

Know Your ABCs

Directions: Write these words in order. If two words start with the same letter, look at the second letter in each word.

Example: lamb   Lamb comes first because **a** comes
          light   before **i** in the alphabet.

tree   _____

branch   _____

leaf   _____

dish   _____

dog   _____

bone   _____

rain   _____

umbrella _____

cloud   _____

mail   _____

stamp   _____

slot   _____

From A to Z

If the first letters of two words are the same, look at the second letters in both words. If the second letters are the same, look at the third letters.

Directions: Write 1, 2, 3 or 4 on the lines in each row to put the words in ABC order.

Example:

1. __1__ candy __2__ carrot __4__ duck __3__ dance

2. ____ cold ____ hot ____ carry ____ hit

3. ____ flash ____ fan ____ fun ____ garden

4. ____ seat ____ sun ____ saw ____ sit

5. ____ row ____ ring ____ rock ____ run

6. ____ truck ____ turn ____ twin ____ talk

Friends and Family

Directions: Write the following names in ABC order:
Oscar, Ali, Lance, Kim, Zane and Bonita.

Directions: Write the names of six of your friends or
family in ABC order.

Super Similar

Words that mean the same or nearly the same are called **synonyms**.

Directions: Read the sentence that tells about the picture. Draw a circle around the word that means the same as the **bold** word.

The child is **unhappy**.

sad   hungry

The flowers are **lovely**.

pretty   green

The baby was very **tired**.

sleepy   hurt

The **funny** clown made us laugh.

silly   glad

The ladybug is so **tiny**.

small   red

We saw a **scary** tiger.

frightening   ugly

A Silly Synonym Story

Synonyms are words that have almost the same meaning.

Directions: Read the story. Then, fill in the blanks with the synonyms.

funny   unhappy

windy   little

A New Balloon

It was a breezy day. The wind blew the small child's balloon away. The child was sad. A silly clown gave him a new balloon.

1. It was a _____ day.

2. The wind blew the _____ child's balloon away.

3. The child was _____.

4. A _____ clown gave him a new balloon.

So Many Synonyms!

Directions: Read each sentence. Fill in the blanks with the synonyms.

| friend | tired | story | presents | little |

I want to go to bed because I am very <u>sleepy</u>.

_____

On my birthday I like to open my <u>gifts</u>.

_____

My <u>pal</u> and I like to play together.

_____

My favorite <u>tale</u> is *Cinderella*.

_____

The mouse was so <u>tiny</u> that it was hard to catch him.

_____

All About Antonyms

Antonyms are words that mean the opposite of another word.

Examples:

hot and **cold**
short and **tall**

Directions: Draw a line from each word on the left to its antonym on the right.

sad	white
bottom	stop
black	fat
tall	top
thin	hard
little	found
cold	short
lost	hot
go	big
soft	happy

Spotty on the Go

Directions: Read the sentences. Complete each sentence with the correct antonym. Use the clues in the picture and below each sentence. Then, color the picture.

1. Spotty's suitcase is ____ .
   (antonym for closed)

   _____

2. Spotty has a ____ on his face.
   (antonym for frown)

   _____

3. His pillow is ____ .
   (antonym for hard)

   _____

4. His coat is ____ .
   (antonym for little)

   _____

5. Spotty packs his stuffed animal ____ .
   (antonym for first)

   _____

Hearing Homophones

Homophones are words that sound the same but are spelled differently and mean different things.

Directions: Write the homophone from the box next to each picture.

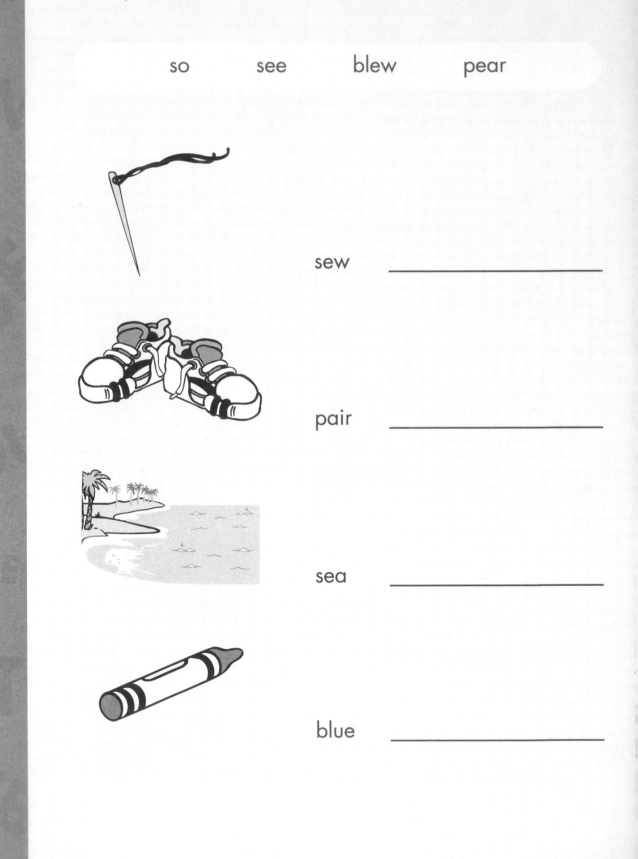

| so | see | blew | pear |

sew _____

pair _____

sea _____

blue _____

Which One's Which?

Directions: Look at each picture. Circle the correct homophone.

deer   dear

blue   blew

two   to

hi   high

by   bye

new   knew

Nouns I Know

A noun is the name of a person, place or thing.

Directions: Read the story and circle all the nouns. Then, write the nouns next to the pictures below.

Our family likes to go to the park.

_____

_____

We play on the swings.

_____

We eat cake.

_____

We drink lemonade.

_____

We throw the ball to our dog.

_____

_____

Then, we go home.

_____

Nouns All Around

Directions: Look through a magazine. Cut out pictures of nouns and glue them below. Write the name of the noun next to the picture.

Nouns

Name-It Nouns

Proper nouns are the names of specific people, places and pets. Proper nouns begin with a capital letter.

Directions: Write the proper nouns on the lines below. Use capital letters at the beginning of each word.

logan, utah

mike smith

_____

_____

lynn cramer

buster

_____

_____

fluffy

chicago, illinois

_____

_____

It's a Date!

The days of the week and the months of the year are always capitalized.

Directions: Circle the words that are written correctly. Write the words that need capital letters on the lines below.

sunday	July	Wednesday
may	december	friday
tuesday	june	august
Monday	january	February
March	Thursday	April
September	saturday	October

Days of the Week   **Months of the Year**

1. _____   1. _____

2. _____   2. _____

3. _____   3. _____

4. _____   4. _____

                              5. _____

A Capital Idea

The first word and all of the important words in a title begin with a capital letter.

Directions: Write the book titles on the lines below. Use capital letters.

1. _____

2. _____

3. _____

4. _____

5. _____

6. _____

A Number of Nouns

Plural nouns name more than one person, place or thing.

Directions: Read the words in the box. Write the words in the correct column.

hats	girl	cows	kittens	cake
spoons	glass	book	horse	trees

one

more than one

_____   _____

_____   _____

_____   _____

_____   _____

_____   _____

Plenty of Plurals

Plurals are words that mean more than one. You usually add an **s** or **es** to the word. In some words ending in **y**, the **y** changes to an **i** before adding **es**. For example, **baby** changes to **babies**.

Directions: Look at the following lists of plural words. Write the word that means one next to it. The first one has been done for you.

foxes ___fox___   balls _____

bushes _____   candies _____

dresses _____   wishes _____

chairs _____   boxes _____

shoes _____   ladies _____

stories _____   bunnies _____

puppies _____   desks _____

matches _____   dishes _____

Pronoun Pros

Pronouns are words that can be used instead of nouns. **She**, **he**, **it** and **they** are pronouns.

Directions: Read the sentence. Then, write the sentence again, using **she**, **he**, **it** or **they** in the blank.

1. Dan likes funny jokes.

_____ likes funny jokes.

2. Peg and Sam went to the zoo.

_____ went to the zoo.

3. My dog likes to dig in the yard.

_____ likes to dig in the yard.

4. Sara is a very good dancer.

_____ is a very good dancer.

5. Fred and Ted are twins.

_____ are twins.

What's It All About?

The **subject** of a sentence is the person, place or thing the sentence is about.

Directions: Underline the subject in each sentence.

Example: Mom read a book.
(Think: Who is the sentence about? <u>Mom</u>)

1. The bird flew away.

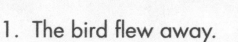

2. The kite was high in the air.

3. The children played a game.

4. The books fell down.

5. The monkey climbed a tree.

Double Up

Two similar sentences can be joined into one sentence if the predicate is the same. A **compound subject** is made up of two subjects joined together by the word **and**.

Example: Jamie can sing.

Sandy can sing.

Jamie **and** Sandy can sing.

Directions: Combine the sentences. Write the new sentence on the line.

1. The cats are my pets.
   The dogs are my pets.

   _____

   _____

2. Chairs are in the store.
   Tables are in the store.

   _____

   _____

3. Tom can ride a bike.
   Jack can ride a bike.

   _____

   _____

Play Ball!

A **verb** is the action word in a sentence. Verbs tell what something does or that something exists.

Example: Run, **sleep** and **jump** are verbs.

Directions: Circle the verbs in the sentences below.

1. We play baseball everyday.

2. Susan pitches the ball very well.

3. Mike swings the bat harder than anyone.

4. Chris slides into home base.

5. Laura hit a home run.

Verb Alert!

We use verbs to tell when something happens.
Sometimes we add an **ed** to verbs that tell us if
something has already happened.

Example: Today, we will **play**. Yesterday, we **played**.

Directions: Write the correct verb in the blank.

1. Today, I will _____ my dog, Fritz.
   wash   washed

2. Last week, Fritz _____ when we
   cry   cried

   said, "Bath time, Fritz."

3. My sister likes to _____ wash Fritz.
   help   helped

4. One time she _____ Fritz
   by herself.   clean   cleaned

5. Fritz will _____ a lot better after
   his bath.   look   looked

Predicate Power

The **predicate** is the part of the sentence that tells about the action.

Directions: Circle the predicate in each sentence.

Example: The boys ran on the playground.

(Think: The boys did what? (Ran))

1. The woman painted a picture.

2. The puppy chases his ball.

3. The students went to school.

4. Butterflies fly in the air.

5. The baby wants a drink.

Twice the Action

A **compound predicate** is made by joining two sentences that have the same subject. The predicates are joined together by the word **and**.

Example: Tom can jump.

Tom can run.

Tom can run **and** jump.

Directions: Combine the sentences. Write the new sentence on the line.

1. The dog can roll over.
   The dog can bark.

_____

_____

2. My mom plays with me.
   My mom reads with me.

_____

_____

3. Tara is tall.
   Tara is smart.

_____

_____

School Days

The **subject** part of the sentence is the person, place or thing the sentence is about. The **predicate** is the part of the sentence that tells what the subject does.

Directions: Draw a line between the subject and the predicate. Underline the noun in the subject and circle the verb.

Example: The furry <u>cat</u> | (ate) food.

1. Mandi walks to school.

2. The bus drove the children.

3. The school bell rang very loudly.

4. The teacher spoke to the students.

5. The girls opened their books.

All Together Now

Directions: Write one new sentence using a compound subject or predicate.

Example: The boy will jump. The girl will jump.

The <u>boy and girl</u> will jump.

1. The clowns run. The clowns play.

_____

_____

2. The dogs dance. The bears dance.

_____

_____

3. Seals bark. Seals clap.

_____

_____

4. The girls play. The girls laugh.

_____

_____

Ready to Roll

Directions: Draw a circle around the noun, the naming part of the sentence. Draw a line under the verb, the action part of the sentence.

Example: (John) <u>drinks</u> juice every morning.

1. Our class skates at the roller-skating rink.

2. Miguel and Emma go very fast.

3. Austin eats hot dogs.

4. Sierra dances to the music.

5. Everyone likes the skating rink.

Tell Me More!

Adjectives are words that tell more about a person, place or thing.

Examples: cold, fuzzy, dark

Directions: Circle the adjectives in the sentences.

1. The juicy apple is on the plate.

2. The furry dog is eating a bone.

3. It was a sunny day.

4. The kitten drinks warm milk.

5. The baby has a loud cry.

A Day on the Farm

Directions: Choose an adjective from the box to fill in the blanks.

hungry	sunny	busy	funny
fresh	deep	pretty	cloudy

1. It is a _____ day on Farmer Brown's farm.

2. Farmer Brown is a very _____ man.

3. Mrs. Brown likes to feed the _____ chickens.

4. Every day she collects the _____ eggs.

5. The ducks swim in the _____ pond.

Make a Wish!

Articles are small words that help us to better understand nouns. **A** and **an** are articles. We use **an** before a word that begins with a vowel. We use a before **a** word that begins with a consonant.

Example: We looked in **a** nest. It had **an** eagle in it.

Directions: Read the sentences. Write **a** or **an** in the blank.

1. 1. I found _____ book.

2. It had a story about _____ ant in it.

3. In the story, _____ lion gave three wishes to ant.

4. The ant's first wish was to ride _____ elephant.

5. The second wish was to ride _____ alligator.

6. The last wish was _____ wish for three more wishes.

Sentence Sense

A **sentence** tells a complete idea. It has a noun and a verb. It begins with a capital letter and has punctuation at the end.

Directions: Circle the group of words if it is a sentence.

1. Grass is a green plant.

2. Mowing the lawn.

3. Grass grows in fields and lawns.

4. Tickle the feet.

5. Sheep, cows and horses eat grass.

6. We like to play in.

7. My sister likes to mow the lawn.

8. A picnic on the grass.

Making a Statement

Statements are sentences that tell us something. They begin with a capital letter and end with a period.

Directions: Write the sentences on the lines below. Begin each sentence with a capital letter and end it with a period.

1. we like to ride our bikes

_____

_____

2. we go down the hill very fast

_____

_____

3. we keep our bikes shiny and clean

_____

_____

4. we know how to change the tires

_____

_____

Ask Me a Question

Questions are sentences that ask something. They begin with a capital letter and end with a question mark.

Directions: Write the questions on the lines below. Begin each sentence with a capital letter and end it with a question mark.

1. will you be my friend

_____

_____

2. what is your name

_____

_____

3. are you eight years old

_____

_____

4. do you like rainbows

_____

_____

What a Surprise!

Surprising sentences tell a strong feeling and end with an exclamation point. A surprising sentence may be only one or two words showing fear, surprise or pain.
Example: Oh, no!

Directions: Put a period at the end of the sentences that tell something. Put an exclamation point at the end of the sentences that tell a strong feeling. Put a question mark at the end of the sentences that ask a question.

1. The cheetah can run very fast

2. Wow

3. Look at that cheetah go

4. Can you run fast

5. Oh, my

6. You're faster than I am

7. Let's run together

8. We can run as fast as a cheetah

9. What fun

10. Do you think cheetahs get tired

That's Mine!

We add **'s** to nouns (people, places or things) to tell who or what owns something.

Directions: Read the sentences. Fill in the blanks to show ownership.

Example: The doll belongs to **Sara**.

It is **Sara's** doll.

1. Sparky has a red collar.

   _____ collar is red.

2. Jimmy has a blue coat.

   _____ coat is blue.

3. The tail of the cat is short.

   The _____ tail is short.

4. The name of my mother is Karen.

   My _____ name is Karen.

Owning Up

Directions: Read the sentences. Choose the correct word and write it in the sentences below.

1. The _____ lunchbox is broken.

   boys   boy's

2. The _____ played in the cage.

   gerbil's   gerbils

3. _____ hair is brown.

   Anns   Ann's

4. The _____ ran in the field.

   horse's   horses

5. My _____ coat is torn.

   sister's   sisters

6. The _____ fur is brown.

   cats   cat's

7. Three _____ flew past our window.

   birds   bird's

8. The _____ paws are muddy.

   dogs   dog's

Look It Up

A dictionary is a book that gives the meaning of words. It also tells how words sound. Words in a dictionary are in ABC order. That makes them easier to find. A picture dictionary lists a word, a picture of the word and its meaning.

Directions: Look at this page from a picture dictionary. Then, answer the questions.

baby

A very young child.

band

A group of people who play music.

bank

A place where money is kept.

bark

The sound a dog makes.

berry

A small, juicy fruit.

board

A flat piece of wood.

1. What is a small, juicy fruit? _____

2. What is a group of people who play music? _____

3. What is the name for a very young child? _____

4. What is a flat piece of wood called? _____

Word to Word

The guide words at the top of a page in a dictionary tell you what the first and last words on the page will be. Only words that come in ABC order between those two words will be on that page. Guide words help you find the page you need to look up a word.

Directions: Write each word from the box in ABC order between each pair of guide words.

faint	far	fence	feed	farmer
fan	feet	farm	family	face

face   **fence**

_____   _____

_____   _____

_____   _____

_____   _____

_____   _____

Many Meanings

When words have more than one meaning, the meanings are numbered in a dictionary.

Directions: Read the meanings of **tag**. Write the number of the correct definition after each sentence.

tag

1. A small strip or tab attached to something else.

2. To label.

3. To follow closely and constantly.

4. A game of chase.

1. We will play a game of tag after we study. _____

2. I will tag this coat with its price. _____

3. My little brother will tag along with us. _____

4. My mother already took off the price tag. _____

5. The tag on the puppy said, "For Sale." _____

6. Do not tag that tree. _____

Number Names

Directions: Write each number word beside the correct picture. Then, write it again.

Example:

six   six

one two three four five six seven eight nine ten

_____

_____

_____

_____

_____

_____

_____

_____

_____

Say It With Numbers

Directions: Change the telling sentences into asking sentences. Change the asking sentences into telling sentences. Begin each one with a capital letter and end it with a period or a question mark.

Examples:

Is she eating three cookies?

<u>She is eating three cookies.</u>

He is bringing one truck.

<u>Is he bringing one truck?</u>

1. Is he painting two bluebirds?

_____

_____

2. Did she find four apples?

_____

_____

3. She will be six on her birthday.

_____

_____

Super Sounds: Short a

Directions: Use a word from the box to complete each sentence.

fat	path	lamp	can
van	stamp	Dan	math
sat	cat	fan	bat

Example:

1. The _____ lamp _____ had a pink shade.

2. The bike _____ led us to the park.

3. I like to add in _____ class.

4. The cat is very _____ .

5. The _____ of beans was hard to open.

6. The envelope needed a _____ .

7. He swung the _____ and hit the ball.

8. The _____ blew air around.

9. My mom drives a blue _____ .

10. I _____ in the backseat.

Super Sounds: Long a

Long a is the vowel sound which says its own name.
Long a can be spelled **ai** as in the word **mail**, **ay** as in the word **say** and **a** with a **silent e** at the end of a word as in the word **same**.

Directions: Say each word and listen for the **long a** sound. Then, write each word and underline the letters that make the **long a** vowel sound.

mail	bake	train
game	day	sale
paint	play	name
made	gray	tray

1. _____

2. _____

3. _____

4. _____

5. _____

6. _____

7. _____

8. _____

9. _____

10. _____

11. _____

12. _____

Super Sounds: Short e

Directions: Write the correct short e word in each sentence.

| get | Meg | rest | bed | spent |
| test | head | pet | red | best |

1. Of all my crayons, I like the _____

   color the _____!

2. I always make my _____ when I

   _____ up.

3. My new hat keeps my _____
   warm.

4. _____ wanted a dog

   for a _____.

5. I have a _____ in math tomorrow,

   so I want to get a good night's _____.

Super Sounds: Long e

Long e is the vowel sound which says its own name.
Long e can be spelled **ee** as in the word **teeth**, **ea** as
in the word **meat** or **e** as in the word **me**.

Directions: Say each word and listen for the **long e**
sound. Then, write the words and underline the letters
that make the **long e** sound.

street	neat	treat
feet	sleep	keep
deal	meal	mean
clean	beast	feast

1. _____

2. _____

3. _____

4. _____

5. _____

6. _____

7. _____

8. _____

9. _____

10. _____

11. _____

12. _____

Super Sounds: Short i

Short i is the sound you hear in the word **pin**.

Directions: Use the **short i** words in the box to write rhyming words.

pin	fin	win	fish
pitch	wish	rich	kick
ship	dip	dish	sick

1. Write the words that rhyme with **spin**.

   _____ _____ _____

2. Write the words that rhyme with **ditch**.

   _____ _____

3. Write the words that rhyme with **rip**.

   _____ _____

4. Write the words that rhyme with **squish**.

   _____ _____ _____

5. Write the words that rhyme with **lick**.

   _____ _____

Super Sounds: Long i

Long i is the vowel sound which says its own name. **Long i** can be spelled **igh** as in **sight**, **i** with a **silent e** at the end as in **mine** and **y** at the end as in **fly**.

Directions: Say each word and listen for the **long i** sound. Then, write each word and underline the letters that make the **long i** sound.

bike	hike	ride
line	glide	ripe
nine	pipe	fight
high	light	sigh

1. _____

2. _____

3. _____

4. _____

5. _____

6. _____

7. _____

8. _____

9. _____

10. _____

11. _____

12. _____

Super Sounds: Short o

Short o is the vowel sound you hear in the word **got**.

Directions: Use the **short o** words in the box to write rhyming words.

hot	rock
lock	cot
stop	sock
fox	mop
box	clock

1. Write the words that rhyme with **dot**.

   _____   _____

2. Write the words that rhyme with **socks**.

   _____   _____

3. Write the words that rhyme with **hop**.

   _____   _____

4. Write the words that rhyme with **dock**.

   _____   _____

   _____   _____

Super Sounds: Long o

Directions: Draw a line from the first part of the sentence to the part which completes the sentence.

1. Do you know   in the water.

2. The dog   was in the tree.

3. The boat floats   who wrote the note?

4. I hope the phone   has a bone.

5. Carol's ice-cream cone   rings soon for me!

6. The rope swing   a coat in the cold.

7. I had to wear   was melting.

Super Sounds: Short u

Directions: Circle the words in each sentence which are not correct. Then, write the correct **short u** words from the box on the lines.

tub	cub	bump
pump	bug	dust
cut	must	nut
jump	rug	hug

1. The crust made me sneeze.

   _____

2. I need to take a bath in the cub.

   _____

3. The mug bite left a big pump on my arm.

   _____ _____

4. It is time to get my hair hut.

   _____

5. The mother bear took care of her shrub.

   _____

6. We need to jump more gas into the car.

   _____

Super Sounds: Long u

Long u is the vowel sound you hear in the word **cube**. Another vowel sound which is very much like the **long u** sound is the **oo** sound you hear in the word **boot**.

Directions: Use the **long u** and **oo** words in the box to write rhyming words.

moon	use	blew
flew	loose	choose
fuse	noon	goose

1. Write the words that rhyme with **soon**.

   _____   _____

2. Write the words that rhyme with **lose**.

   _____   _____   _____

3. Write the words that rhyme with **grew**.

   _____   _____

4. Write the words that rhyme with **moose**.

   _____   _____

Ready, Set, Action!

Verbs are words that tell the action in the sentence.

Directions: Draw a line from each sentence to its picture. Then, finish the sentence with the verb or action word that is under each picture.

Example:

He will _____ help _____ the baby.

carry

1. I can _____ my book.

help

2. It is time to _____ up.

cut

3. That chair might _____.

build

4. They _____ houses.

clean

5. I _____ this out myself.

fix

6. Is that too heavy to _____?

break

How Does It End?

Most **verbs** end with **s** when the sentence tells about one thing. The **s** is taken away when the sentence tells about more than one thing.

Example:

One dog walks.   One boy runs.
Two dogs **walk**.   Three boys **run**.

The spelling of some **verbs** changes when the sentence tells about only one thing.

One girl carries her lunch.   The boy fixes his car.
Two girls **carry** their lunches.   The boys **fix** their cars.

Directions: Write the missing verbs in the sentences.

Example:

Pam works hard. She and Peter _____work_____ all day.

1. The father bird builds a nest.

   The mother and father _____ it together.

2. The girls clean their room.

   Jenny _____ under her bed.

3. The children cut out their pictures.

   Henry _____ his slowly.

4. These workers fix things.

   This man _____ televisions.

5. Two trucks carry horses.

   One truck _____ pigs.

Animal Action

Directions: Circle the word in each sentence that is not spelled correctly. Then, write it correctly.

> squirrel   bears   rabbit   deer   fox   mouse

Example:

Animals like to live in (threes.)   <u>   trees   </u>

1. Bares do not eat people.   _____

2. The squirel found a nut.   _____

3. Sometimes a little moose might get into your house.   _____

4. Dear eat leaves and grass.   _____

5. A focks has a bushy tail.   _____

6. One day, a rabitt came into our yard.   _____

Lots of Animals

Directions: Write the two sentences below as one sentence. Remember the special spelling of **fox**, **mouse** and **deer** when there are more than one.

Example:

I saw a mouse. You saw a mouse.

We saw two mice.

1. Julie petted a deer.
   Matt petted a deer.

   _____

   _____

2. Mike colored a fox.
   Kim colored a fox.

   _____

   _____

All in the Family

Directions: This is Andy's **family tree**. It shows all the people in his family. Use the words in the box to finish writing the names in Andy's family tree.

grandmother	mother
grandfather	father
aunt	uncle
brother	sister

grandmother   grandfather   _____   _____

aunt   _____   my mother   my father   _____   uncle

sister   brother   me – Andy   _____   _____

Once Upon a Family

Directions: Write the family words in the blanks to complete the story.

One day, my family had a picnic. My

_____ baked chicken.

_____ baked some rolls.

My _____ Jack brought corn. My

_____ made something green and

white in a big dish. I ate the chicken my

_____ brought. I had two rolls made

by my _____. My _____

gave me some corn. I liked it all! Then, my

_____ and I looked in the dish my

_____ had brought. "Did you try it?"

I asked him.

"You're my big _____," he said.

"You try it!" I put a tiny bit in my mouth. It tasted good!

But the dish was almost empty.

"It's terrible!" I said. "I'll eat the rest of it so you

won't have to. That's what a big _____

is for!" My _____ watched me eat it all.

I tried not to look too happy!

Where in the World?

Directions: Draw a line from each sentence to its picture. Then, complete each sentence with the word under the picture.

Example:

He is walking ___behind___ the tree.

outside

1. We stay _____ when it rains.

behind

2. She drew a dog _____ his house.

between

3. She stands _____ her friends.

across

4. They walked _____ the bridge.

around

5. Let the cat go _____.

beside

6. Draw a circle _____ the fish.

inside

Find That Cat!

Directions: Use a location word to tell where the cat is in each sentence.

Example:

The cat is behind the box.

_____

_____

_____

_____

_____

_____

_____

_____

Heads or Tails?

Directions: Opposites are words which are different in every way. Use the opposite word from the box to complete these sentences.

| hard | hot | bottom | quickly | happy |
| sad | slowly | cold | soft | top |

Example:

My new coat is blue on _____top_____ and

red on the ___bottom___.

1. Snow is _____, but fire is _____.

2. A rabbit runs _____, but a turtle

   moves _____.

3. A bed is _____, but a floor

   is _____.

4. I feel _____ when my friends come

   and _____ when they leave.

A Sweet Surprise

Directions: Write opposite words in the blanks to complete the story.

> hot   hard   top   cold   slowly
>
> soft   quickly   happy   bottom   sad

One day, Grandma came for a visit. She gave my sister Jenny and me a box of chocolate candy. We said, "Thank you!" Then, Jenny _____ took the _____ off the box. The pieces all looked the same! I couldn't tell which pieces were _____ inside and which were _____! I only liked the _____ ones. Jenny didn't care. She was _____ to get any kind of candy!

I _____ looked at all the pieces. I didn't know which one to pick. Just then Dad called us. Grandma was going home. He wanted us to say good-bye to her. I hurried to the front door where they were standing. Jenny came a minute later.

I told Grandma I hoped I would see her soon. I always feel _____ when she leaves. Jenny stood behind me and didn't say anything. After Grandma went home, I found out why. Jenny had most of our candy in her mouth! Only a few pieces were left in the _____ of the box! Then, I was _____! That Jenny!

Tick, Tock, Time

The time between breakfast and lunch is **morning**.

The time between lunch and dinner is **afternoon**.

The time between dinner and bedtime is **evening**.

Directions: Write a time word from the box to complete each sentence. Use each word only once.

> evening   morning   today   tomorrow   afternoon

1. What did you eat for breakfast

   this _____?

2. We came home from school in

   the _____.

3. I help wash the dinner dishes in

   the _____.

4. I feel a little tired _____.

5. If I rest tonight, I will feel

   better _____.

What Time Is It?

Directions: Write a sentence for these time words. Tell something you do at that time.

Example:

day

<u>Every day I walk to school.</u>

morning

_____

_____

afternoon

_____

_____

evening

_____

_____

Review

Directions: Write the story below again and correct all the mistakes. Watch for words that are not spelled correctly, missing periods and question marks, question marks at the end of telling sentences and sentences with the wrong joining words.

One mourning, my granmother said I could have a pet mouse. That evenening, we got my mouse at the pet store, or the next afernoon my mouse had babies! Now, I had nyne mouses! I really liked to wach them? I wanted to pick the babies up, and they were too little. When they get bigger, I have to give too mouses to my sisster.

_____

_____

_____

_____

_____

_____

_____

_____

_____

_____

Math

Shape Escape!

Directions: Complete each row by drawing the correct shape.

Pick a Pattern

Mia likes to count by twos, threes, fours, fives, tens and hundreds.

1 2 3 4 5

Directions: Complete the number patterns.

1. 5, ____, ____, 20, ____, ____, 35, ____, ____, 50

2. 100, ____, ____, 400, ____, ____, ____, 800, ____

3. ____, 4, 6, ____, ____, 12, ____, 16, ____, ____

4. 10, ____, ____, 40, ____, ____, 70, ____, 90

5. 4, ____, 12, ____, ____, 24, ____, 32, ____, 40

Directions: Make up two of your own number patterns.

____, ____, ____, ____, ____, ____, ____, ____

____, ____, ____, ____, ____, ____, ____, ____

All Aboard!

Ordinal numbers indicate order in a series, such as **first**, **second** or **third**.

Directions: Follow the instructions to color the train cars. The first car is the engine.

Color the third car **blue**.

Color the eighth car green.

Color the fifth car orange.

Color the sixth car yellow.

Color the fourth car **brown**.

Color the second car **purple**.

Color the first car **red**.

Color the seventh car pink.

Add Attack!

Addition is "putting together" or adding two or more numbers to find the sum.

Directions: Add.

Example:

$$\begin{array}{r} 2 \\ +5 \\ \hline 7 \end{array}$$

$$\begin{array}{r} 3 \\ +4 \\ \hline \end{array}$$
$$\begin{array}{r} 6 \\ +2 \\ \hline \end{array}$$
$$\begin{array}{r} 7 \\ +1 \\ \hline \end{array}$$
$$\begin{array}{r} 8 \\ +2 \\ \hline \end{array}$$
$$\begin{array}{r} 5 \\ +4 \\ \hline \end{array}$$

$$\begin{array}{r} 8 \\ +2 \\ \hline \end{array}$$
$$\begin{array}{r} 9 \\ +5 \\ \hline \end{array}$$
$$\begin{array}{r} 10 \\ +3 \\ \hline \end{array}$$
$$\begin{array}{r} 6 \\ +6 \\ \hline \end{array}$$
$$\begin{array}{r} 4 \\ +9 \\ \hline \end{array}$$

$$\begin{array}{r} 9 \\ +3 \\ \hline \end{array}$$
$$\begin{array}{r} 8 \\ +7 \\ \hline \end{array}$$
$$\begin{array}{r} 6 \\ +5 \\ \hline \end{array}$$
$$\begin{array}{r} 7 \\ +9 \\ \hline \end{array}$$
$$\begin{array}{r} 7 \\ +6 \\ \hline \end{array}$$

Add Attack: Forward and Back

The commutative property of addition states that even if the order of the numbers is changed in an addition sentence, the sum will stay tye same.

Example: 2 + 3 = 5
3 + 2 = 5

Directions: Look at the addition sentences below. Complete the addition sentences by writing the missing numerals.

5 + 4 = 9   3 + 1 = 4

4 + __ = 9   1 + __ = 4

2 + 6 = 8   6 + 1 = 7

6 + __ = 8   1 + __ = 7

Now try these:

6 + 3 = 9   10 + 2 = 12

__ + __ = 9   __ + __ = 12

Look at these sums. Can you think of two number sentences that would show the commutative property of addition.

__ + __ = 7   __ + __ = 11

__ + __ = 7   __ + __ = 11

Add Attack: 3 or More Numbers

Directions: Add all the numbers to find the sum. Draw pictures to help or break up the problem into two smaller problems.

Example:

$$\begin{array}{r} 3 \\ 6 \\ +2 \\ \hline \end{array} \qquad \begin{array}{r} 8 \\ 5 \\ +4 \\ \hline \end{array} \qquad \begin{array}{r} 3 \\ 1 \\ +5 \\ \hline \end{array} \qquad \begin{array}{r} 8 \\ 2 \\ +9 \\ \hline \end{array}$$

$$\begin{array}{r} 2 \\ 8 \\ 4 \\ +3 \\ \hline \end{array} \qquad \begin{array}{r} 3 \\ 6 \\ 5 \\ +2 \\ \hline \end{array} \qquad \begin{array}{r} 4 \\ 1 \\ 2 \\ +5 \\ \hline \end{array} \qquad \begin{array}{r} 6 \\ 7 \\ 3 \\ +1 \\ \hline \end{array}$$

Take It Away!

Subtraction is "taking away" or subtracting one number from another to find the difference.

Directions: Subtract.

Example:

$$\begin{array}{r} 4 \\ -3 \\ \hline 1 \end{array}$$

$$\begin{array}{r} 5 \\ -3 \\ \hline \end{array} \qquad \begin{array}{r} 6 \\ -1 \\ \hline \end{array} \qquad \begin{array}{r} 4 \\ -3 \\ \hline \end{array} \qquad \begin{array}{r} 3 \\ -1 \\ \hline \end{array} \qquad \begin{array}{r} 2 \\ -0 \\ \hline \end{array}$$

$$\begin{array}{r} 9 \\ -2 \\ \hline \end{array} \qquad \begin{array}{r} 7 \\ -4 \\ \hline \end{array} \qquad \begin{array}{r} 10 \\ -5 \\ \hline \end{array} \qquad \begin{array}{r} 14 \\ -6 \\ \hline \end{array} \qquad \begin{array}{r} 15 \\ -9 \\ \hline \end{array}$$

$$\begin{array}{r} 18 \\ -8 \\ \hline \end{array} \qquad \begin{array}{r} 13 \\ -5 \\ \hline \end{array} \qquad \begin{array}{r} 14 \\ -7 \\ \hline \end{array} \qquad \begin{array}{r} 11 \\ -4 \\ \hline \end{array} \qquad \begin{array}{r} 17 \\ -9 \\ \hline \end{array}$$

Find Your Place

The place value of a digit or numeral is shown by where it is in the number. For example, in the number **23**, **2** has the place value of **tens**, and **3** is **ones**.

Directions: Add the tens and ones and write your answers in the blanks.

Example:

3 tens   +   3 ones   =   **33**

tens ones   **tens ones**

7 tens + 5 ones = _____   4 tens + 0 ones = _____

2 tens + 3 ones = _____   8 tens + 1 one = _____

5 tens + 2 ones = _____   1 ten + 1 one = _____

5 tens + 4 ones = _____   6 tens + 3 ones = _____

Directions: Draw a line to the correct number.

6 tens   +   7 ones   73

4 tens   +   2 ones   67

8 tens   +   0 ones   51

7 tens   +   3 ones   80

5 tens   +   1 one   42

Add Attack: 2 Digits

Directions: Study the example. Follow the steps to add.

Example:

$$33$$
$$+41$$

Step 1: Add the ones.   **Step 2:** Add the tens.

24	15	38	11	37
+62	+23	+61	+26	+42

25	62	32	25	82
+42	+14	+44	+13	+ 6

Add Attack: 2 Digits

Directions: Add the total points scored in each game. Remember to add **ones** first and **tens** second.

Example:

Total _____39_____

HOME 28
VISITOR 30

Total _____

HOME 55
VISITOR 21

Total _____

HOME 14
VISITOR 33

Total _____

HOME 24
VISITOR 13

Total _____

HOME 46
VISITOR 32

Total _____

HOME 83
VISITOR 06

Total _____

HOME 30
VISITOR 20

Total _____

HOME 17
VISITOR 42

Total _____

HOME 24
VISITOR 45

Total _____

Add Attack: 2 Digits

Addition is "putting together" or adding two or more numbers to find the sum. Regrouping is using **ten ones** to form **one ten**, **ten tens** to form **one 100**, **fifteen ones** to form **one ten** and **five ones** and so on.

Directions: Study the examples. Follow the steps to add.

Example:

$$\begin{array}{r} 14 \\ +8 \\ \hline \end{array}$$

Step 1:
Add the ones.

Step 2:
Regroup the tens.

Step 3:
Add the tens.

tens	ones
1	
1	6
+3	7
5	3

tens	ones
1	
3	8
+5	3
9	1

tens	ones
1	
2	4
+4	7
7	1

$$\begin{array}{r} 28 \\ +17 \\ \hline \end{array} \qquad \begin{array}{r} 32 \\ +38 \\ \hline \end{array} \qquad \begin{array}{r} 54 \\ +25 \\ \hline \end{array} \qquad \begin{array}{r} 19 \\ +55 \\ \hline \end{array} \qquad \begin{array}{r} 44 \\ +48 \\ \hline \end{array}$$

Add Attack: 2 Digits

Directions: Add the total points scored in the game. Remember to add the ones, regroup, and then add the tens.

Example:

Total ___85___

HOME 33
VISITOR 57

Total _____

HOME 43
VISITOR 49

Total _____

HOME 57
VISITOR 34

Total _____

HOME 29
VISITOR 22

Total _____

HOME 36
VISITOR 58

Total _____

HOME 45
VISITOR 39

Total _____

HOME 66
VISITOR 26

Total _____

HOME 72
VISITOR 19

Total _____

HOME 54
VISITOR 26

Total _____

Take It Away: 2 Digits

Directions: Study the example. Follow the steps to subtract.

Example:

$$\begin{array}{r} 28 \\ -14 \\ \hline \end{array}$$

Step 1: Subtract the ones. **Step 2:** Subtract the tens.

$$\begin{array}{r} 24 \\ -12 \\ \hline \end{array} \qquad \begin{array}{r} 61 \\ -30 \\ \hline \end{array} \qquad \begin{array}{r} 77 \\ -44 \\ \hline \end{array} \qquad \begin{array}{r} 85 \\ -24 \\ \hline \end{array} \qquad \begin{array}{r} 57 \\ -23 \\ \hline \end{array}$$

$$\begin{array}{r} 29 \\ -15 \\ \hline \end{array} \qquad \begin{array}{r} 74 \\ -51 \\ \hline \end{array} \qquad \begin{array}{r} 46 \\ -32 \\ \hline \end{array} \qquad \begin{array}{r} 69 \\ -35 \\ \hline \end{array} \qquad \begin{array}{r} 95 \\ -32 \\ \hline \end{array}$$

Take It Away: 2 Digits

Directions: Study the steps for subtracting. Solve the problems using the steps.

Steps for Subtracting

1. Do you regroup? Yes, when the bottom number is bigger than the top.

2. Subtract the ones.

3. Subtract the tens.

	tens	ones			tens	ones	
	3 ~~4~~	12	Regroup? Yes		3	7	Regroup? No
	− 2	4			− 1	4	
	1	8			2	3	

tens	ones		tens	ones		tens	ones
4	7		6	4		5	3
− 2	8		− 3	4		− 3	9

```
  56        83        43        75        91
 −27       −47       −39       −53       −18
```

```
  73        35        67        26        68
 −66       −14       −58       − 7       −45
```

Review

Directions: Add or subtract. Use regrouping when needed. Always do ones first and tens last.

tens	ones
9	3
-2	5

tens	ones
3	0
+2	7

tens	ones
6	5
+1	7

7	6
-2	8

8	2
+1	9

5	6
-2	8

4	3
-1	4

5	3
-1	5

2	4
+5	7

```
  33
 +47
```

```
  52
 +29
```

```
  46
 -37
```

Hundreds of Places

The place value of a digit or numeral is shown by where it is in the number. For example, in the number **123**, **1** has the place value of **hundreds**, **2** is **tens** and **3** is **ones**.

Directions: Study the examples. Then, write the missing numbers in the blanks.

Examples:

2 hundreds + 3 tens + 6 ones =

hundreds	tens	ones
2	3	6	= _236_

1 hundreds + 4 tens + 9 ones =

hundreds	tens	ones
1	4	9	= _149_

			hundreds	tens	ones	total
3 hundreds +	4 tens +	8 ones =	3	4	8	= _____
___ hundreds +	___ tens +	___ ones =	2	1	7	= _____
___ hundreds +	___ tens +	___ ones =	6	3	5	= _____
___ hundreds +	___ tens +	___ ones =	4	7	9	= _____
___ hundreds +	___ tens +	___ ones =	2	9	4	= _____
___ hundreds +	5 tens +	6 ones =	4	___	___	= _____
3 hundreds +	1 ten +	3 ones =	___	___	___	= _____
3 hundreds +	___ ten +	7 ones =	___	5	___	= _____
6 hundreds +	2 ten +	___ ones =	___	___	8	= _____

Add Attack: 3 Digits

Directions: Study the examples. Follow the steps to add.

Example:

Step 1:
Add the ones.

Do you regroup? Yes

Step 2:
Add the tens.

Do you regroup? No

Step 3:
Add the hundreds.

hundreds	tens	ones
	1	
3	4	8
+4	4	4
		2

hundreds	tens	ones
	1	
3	4	8
+4	4	4
	9	2

hundreds	tens	ones
	1	
3	4	8
+4	4	4
7	9	2

hundreds	tens	ones
	1	
2	1	4
+2	3	8
4	5	2

hundreds	tens	ones
	1	
3	6	8
+2	1	3
___	8	1

hundreds	tens	ones
	1	
1	1	9
+5	6	5
___	___	4

418	471	334	659	736
+323	+319	+528	+127	+145

Add Attack: 3 Digits

Directions: Study the example. Follow the steps to add. Regroup when needed.

Step 1: Add the ones.
Step 2: Add the tens.
Step 3: Add the hundreds.

hundreds	tens	ones
1	1	
3	4	8
+4	5	4
8	0	2

$$10 = 1 \text{ ten} + 0 \text{ ones}$$

$$
\begin{array}{r} 348 \\ +214 \\ \hline \end{array}
\qquad
\begin{array}{r} 172 \\ +418 \\ \hline \end{array}
\qquad
\begin{array}{r} 575 \\ +329 \\ \hline \end{array}
\qquad
\begin{array}{r} 623 \\ +268 \\ \hline \end{array}
\qquad
\begin{array}{r} 369 \\ +533 \\ \hline \end{array}
$$

$$
\begin{array}{r} 411 \\ +299 \\ \hline \end{array}
\qquad
\begin{array}{r} 423 \\ +169 \\ \hline \end{array}
\qquad
\begin{array}{r} 639 \\ +177 \\ \hline \end{array}
\qquad
\begin{array}{r} 624 \\ +368 \\ \hline \end{array}
\qquad
\begin{array}{r} 272 \\ +469 \\ \hline \end{array}
$$

Take It Away: 3 Digits

Directions: Study the example. Follow the steps to subtract.

Step 1: Regroup ones.
Step 2: Subtract ones.
Step 3: Subtract tens.
Step 4: Subtract hundreds.

Example:

hundreds	tens	ones
	5	12
4	6̸	2̸
− 2	5	3
2	0	9

Directions: Draw a line to the correct answer. Color the kites.

347	144	963	762	287
−218	−135	−748	−553	−179

215   209   129   108   9

Take It Away: 3 Digits

Directions: Subtract. Circle the **7**'s that appear in the **tens place**.

score
257

```
 492      184
-221     -129
─────    ─────
 2⑦1
```

```
 358      765      584      693      921
-238     -326     -435     -314     -362
─────    ─────    ─────    ─────    ─────
```

```
 128      744      835      248      635
-109     -674     -217     -199     -428
─────    ─────    ─────    ─────    ─────
```

All in Place

Directions: Study the example. Write the missing numbers.

Example:

1,000   100   10   1
1,000   10   1
               10

2 thousands + 1 hundred + __3__ tens + 2 ones = __2,132__

5,286 = ___ thousands + ___ hundreds + ___ tens + ___ ones

1,831 = ___ thousands + ___ hundreds + ___ tens + ___ ones

8,972 = ___ thousands + ___ hundreds + ___ tens + ___ ones

4,528 = ___ thousands + ___ hundreds + ___ tens + ___ ones

3,177 = ___ thousands + ___ hundreds + ___ tens + ___ ones

Directions: Draw a line to the number that has:

8 hundreds   7,103

5 ones   2,862

9 tens   5,996

7 thousands   1,485

Fan-tastic!

Directions: Use the code to color the fan.

If the answer has:

9 thousands, color it **pink**.
6 thousands, color it green.
5 hundreds, color it orange.
8 tens, color it **red**.
3 ones, color it **blue**.

9,772

81

597

6,370

6,600

6,421 | 9,359

9,727

87

542

9,416

89

4,253

Take a Bite

A graph is a drawing that shows information about numbers.

Directions: Count the apples in each row. Color the boxes to show how many apples have bites taken out of them.

Example:

Something's Fishy!

Directions: Count the fish. Color the bowls to make a graph that shows the number of fish.

Directions: Use your fishbowl graphs to find the answers to the following questions. Draw a line to the correct bowl.

The most fish

The fewest fish

Bunches of Bugs

Multiplication is a short way to find the sum of adding the same number a certain amount of times. For example, **4 x 7 = 28** instead of **7 + 7 + 7 + 7 = 28**.

Directions: Study the example. Solve the problems.

Example:

3 + 3 + 3 = 9

3 threes = 9

3 x 3 = 9

7 + 7 = _____

2 sevens = _____

2 x 7 = _____

4 + 4 + 4 + 4 = _____

4 fours = _____

4 x _____ = _____

5 + 5 = _____

2 fives = _____

2 x _____ = _____

2 + 2 + 2 + 2 = _____

4 twos = _____

4 x _____ = _____

Good Times!

Directions: Study the example. Draw the groups and write the total.

Example:

3 x 2

2 + 2 + 2 = 6

3 x 4

____ + ____ + ____ = _____

2 x 5

____ + ____ = _____

5 x 3

___ + ___ + ___ + ___ + ___ = _____

Focus on Fractions

A fraction is a number that names part of a whole, such as $\frac{1}{2}$ or $\frac{1}{3}$.

Directions: Study the examples. Color the correct fraction of each shape.

Examples:

shaded part   1
equal parts   2
$\frac{1}{2}$ (one-half) shaded

shaded part   1
equal parts   3
$\frac{1}{3}$ (one-third) shaded

shaded part   1
equal parts   4
$\frac{1}{4}$ (one-fourth) shaded

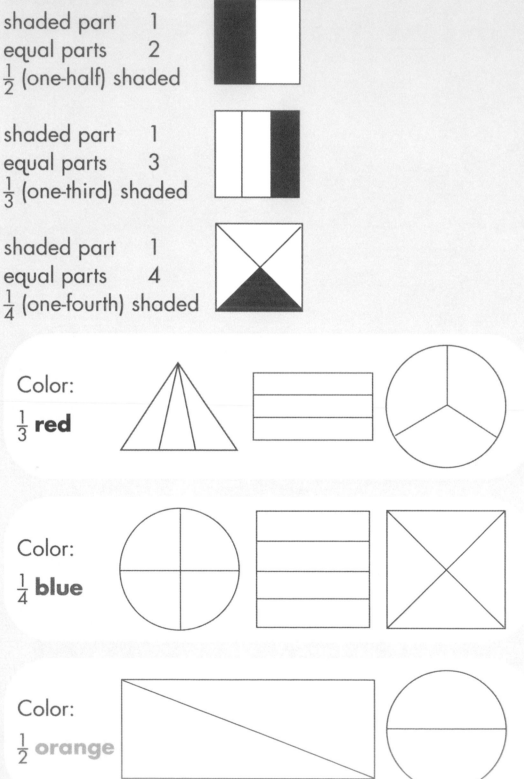

Color:

$\frac{1}{3}$ **red**

Color:

$\frac{1}{4}$ **blue**

Color:

$\frac{1}{2}$ **orange**

Made in the Shade

Directions: Study the examples. Circle the fraction that shows the shaded part. Then, circle the fraction that shows the white part.

Examples:

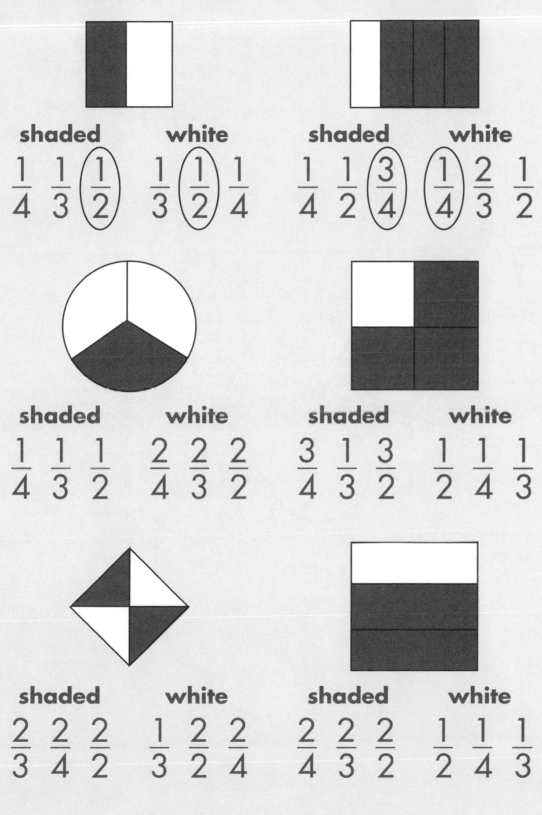

shaded   white   shaded   white

$\frac{1}{4}$ $\frac{1}{3}$ $\boxed{\frac{1}{2}}$ $\frac{1}{3}$ $\boxed{\frac{1}{2}}$ $\frac{1}{4}$ $\frac{1}{4}$ $\frac{1}{2}$ $\boxed{\frac{3}{4}}$ $\boxed{\frac{1}{4}}$ $\frac{2}{3}$ $\frac{1}{2}$

shaded   white   shaded   white

$\frac{1}{4}$ $\frac{1}{3}$ $\frac{1}{2}$ $\frac{2}{4}$ $\frac{2}{3}$ $\frac{2}{2}$ $\frac{3}{4}$ $\frac{1}{3}$ $\frac{3}{2}$ $\frac{1}{2}$ $\frac{1}{4}$ $\frac{1}{3}$

shaded   white   shaded   white

$\frac{2}{3}$ $\frac{2}{4}$ $\frac{2}{2}$ $\frac{1}{3}$ $\frac{2}{2}$ $\frac{2}{4}$ $\frac{2}{4}$ $\frac{2}{3}$ $\frac{2}{2}$ $\frac{1}{2}$ $\frac{1}{4}$ $\frac{1}{3}$

Get in Shape!

Geometry is mathematics that has to do with lines and shapes.

Directions: Color the shapes.

Color the triangles **blue**.

Color the circles **red**.

Color the squares **green**.

Color the rectangles **pink**.

Tangram Tango

Directions: Cut out the tangram below. Mix up the pieces. Try to put it back together into a square.

This page is blank for the cutting activity
on the opposite side.

Measuring Up

Directions: Cut out the ruler. Measure each object to the nearest inch.

_____ inches

_____ inches

_____ inches

Directions: Measure objects around your house. Write the measurement to the nearest inch.

can of soup   _____ inches

pen   _____ inches

toothbrush   _____ inches

paper clip   _____ inches

small toy   _____ inches

cut out

8 7 6 5 4 3 2 1

This page is blank for the cutting activity on the opposite side.

Catch of the Day

Directions: Use the ruler to measure the fish to the nearest inch.

about _____ inches

about _____ inches

about _____ inches

about _____ inches

about _____ inches

about _____ inches

Centimeter Sense

A centimeter is a unit of length in the metric system. There are 2.54 centimeters in an inch.

Directions: Use a centimeter ruler to measure the crayons to the nearest centimeter.

Example: The first crayon is about 7 centimeters long.

about ___7___ centimeters   about _____ centimeters

about _____ centimeters

about _____ centimeters

about _____ centimeters   about _____ centimeters

Hour by Hour

An hour is sixty minutes. The short hand of a clock tells the hour. It is written **0:00**, such as **5:00**. A half-hour is thirty minutes. When the long hand of the clock is pointing to the six, the time is on the half-hour. It is written **:30**, such as **5:30**.

Directions: Study the examples. Tell what time is on each clock.

Examples:

The minute hand is on the 12.
The hour hand is on the 9.
It is 9 o'clock.

9:00

The minute hand is on the 6.
The hour hand is *between* the 4 and 5.
It is 4:30.

4:30

_____   _____   _____   _____

_____   _____   _____   _____

Time's Up!

The minute hand of a clock takes 5 minutes to move from one number to the next. Start at the 12 and count by fives to tell how many minutes it is past the hour.

Directions: Study the examples. Tell what time is on each clock.

Examples:

9:10

8:25

Telling Time

Time can also be shown as fractions. 30 minutes = $\frac{1}{2}$ hour.

Directions: Shade the fraction of each clock and tell how many minutes you have shaded.

Example:

$\frac{1}{2}$ hour

30 minutes

$\frac{1}{4}$ hour

_____ minutes

$\frac{2}{4}$ hour

_____ minutes

$\frac{3}{4}$ hour

_____ minutes

$\frac{1}{2}$ hour

_____ minutes

Review

Counting

Directions: Write the number that is:

next

one less

68, 69, ____

____, 57

786, 787, ____

____, 650

one greater

12, ____

843, ____

Place Value: Tens & Ones

Directions: Draw a line to the correct number.

4 tens + 7 ones   20

2 tens + 0 ones   51

7 tens + 3 ones   47

5 tens + 1 one   73

Addition and Subtraction

Directions: Add or Subtract.

$$\begin{array}{cccc} 15 & 14 & 7 & 8 & 10 \\ +5 & -4 & +3 & -6 & +7 \end{array}$$

Review

2-Digit Addition and Subtraction

Directions: Add or subtract using regrouping, if needed.

66	38	87	52	40
−37	+18	−69	−15	+17

84	65	99	61	56
+17	+14	−48	−36	+46

Place Value: Hundreds and Thousands

Directions: Draw a line to the correct number.

4 hundreds + 3 tens + 2 ones	7,201
6 hundreds + 7 tens + 6 ones	290
5 thousands + 3 hundreds + 7 tens + 2 ones	432
2 hundreds + 9 tens + 0 ones	676
7 thousands + 2 hundreds + 0 tens + 1 one	5,372

3-Digit Addition and Subtraction

Directions: Add or subtract, remembering to regroup, if needed.

458	793	822	528	697
−248	−414	−460	+319	+108

Review

Multiplication

Directions: Solve the problems. Draw groups if necessary.

$$\begin{array}{r} 2 \\ \times 8 \\ \hline \end{array} \qquad \begin{array}{r} 6 \\ \times 4 \\ \hline \end{array} \qquad \begin{array}{r} 3 \\ \times 2 \\ \hline \end{array} \qquad \begin{array}{r} 8 \\ \times 4 \\ \hline \end{array} \qquad \begin{array}{r} 5 \\ \times 3 \\ \hline \end{array}$$

Fractions

Directions: Circle the correct fraction of each shape's white part.

$$\frac{1}{2} \quad \frac{1}{3} \quad \frac{1}{4} \qquad \frac{1}{4} \quad \frac{1}{3} \quad \frac{1}{2} \qquad \frac{2}{3} \quad \frac{2}{4} \quad \frac{1}{3} \qquad \frac{1}{4} \quad \frac{1}{2} \quad \frac{3}{4}$$

Graphs

Directions: Count the flowers. Color the pots to make a graph that shows the number of flowers.

1 2 3 4 5 6 7 8

Review

Geometry

Directions: Match the shapes.

rectangle

square

circle

triangle

Measurement

Directions: Look at the ruler. Measure the objects to the nearest inch.

_____ inches

_____ inches

_____ inches

Time

Directions: Tell what time is on each clock.

_____   _____   _____   _____

It All Makes Cents

Directions: Count the coins and write the amount.

Penny **1¢**   Nickel **5¢**   Dime **10¢**

_____ ¢

_____ ¢

_____ ¢

_____ ¢

_____ ¢

Time for a Change

Directions: Draw a line from the toy to the amount of money it costs.

Counting Coins

A quarter is worth **25¢**.

Directions: Count the coins and write the amounts.

Get to the Point!

A decimal is a number with one or more places to the right of a decimal point, such as 6.5 or 2.25. Money amounts are written with two places to the right of the decimal point.

25¢   10¢   5¢   1¢

$.25 $.10 $.05 $.01

Directions: Count the coins and circle the amount shown.

Example:

($.17)   23¢ $.07 $.50   51¢   61¢

$.28   36¢   42¢   37¢   43¢ $.47

Dollar Days

One dollar equals 100 cents. It is written $1.00.

Directions: Count the money and write the amounts.

$_____ . _____

$_____ . _____

$_____ . _____

$_____ . _____

$_____ . _____

$_____ . _____

$_____ . _____

$_____ . _____

Add It Up

Directions: Write the amount of money using decimals. Then, add to find the total amount.

Example:

$$\$\underline{1}.\underline{0}\,\underline{0}$$
$$\underline{}.\underline{0}\,\underline{5}$$
$$+\underline{}.\underline{0}\,\underline{2}$$
$$\underline{1}.\underline{0}\,\underline{7}$$

$\$\underline{}.\underline{}$
$\$\underline{}.\underline{}$
$\$\underline{}.\underline{}$
$+\$\underline{}.\underline{}$
$\underline{}.\underline{}$

$\$\underline{}.\underline{}$
$\$\underline{}.\underline{}$
$\$\underline{}.\underline{}$
$+\$\underline{}.\underline{}$
$\underline{}.\underline{}$

$\$\underline{}.\underline{}$
$\$\underline{}.\underline{}$
$\$\underline{}.\underline{}$
$+\$\underline{}.\underline{}$
$\underline{}.\underline{}$

$\$\underline{}.\underline{}$
$\$\underline{}.\underline{}$
$\$\underline{}.\underline{}$
$+\$\underline{}.\underline{}$
$\underline{}.\underline{}$

A Day at the Park

Directions: Tell if you add, subtract or multiply. Then, write the answer.

Example:

There were 12 frogs sitting on a log by a pond, but 3 frogs hopped away. How many frogs are left?

<u>Subtract</u>   <u>9</u> frogs

There are 9 flowers growing by the pond. Each flower has 2 leaves. How many leaves are there?

_____ _____ leaves

A tree had 7 squirrels playing in it. Then, 8 more came along. How many squirrels are there in all?

_____ _____ squirrels

There were 27 birds living in the trees around the pond, but 9 flew away. How many birds are left?

_____ _____ birds

Time to Solve It

Directions: Solve each problem.

Tracy wakes up at 7:00. She has
30 minutes before her bus comes.
What time does her bus come?

_____ : _____

Vera walks her dog for 15 minutes
after supper. She finishes supper
at 6:30. When does she get home
from walking her dog?

_____ : _____

Chip practices the piano for 30
minutes when he gets home from
school. He gets home at 3:30.
When does he stop practicing?

_____ : _____

Tanya starts mowing the grass at
4:30. She finishes at 5:00. For
how many minutes does she mow
the lawn?

_____ minutes

Toy Time

Directions: Read each problem. Use the pictures to help you solve the problems.

Ben bought a ball. He had 11¢ left. How much money did he have at the start? _____ ¢

Tara has 75¢. She buys a car. How much money does she have left? _____ ¢

Leah wants to buy a doll and a ball. She has 80¢. How much more money does she need? _____ ¢

Jacob has 95¢. He buys the car and the ball. How much more money does he need to buy a doll for his sister? _____ ¢

Kim paid three quarters, one dime and three pennies for a hat. How much did it cost? _____ ¢

Addition: Putting together or adding two or more numbers to find the sum.

Adjectives: Words that tell more about a person, place or thing.

Alphabetical (ABC) Order: Putting letters or words in the order in which they appear in the alphabet.

Antonyms: Words that mean the opposite. Example: big and small.

Articles: Small words that help us to better understand nouns. Example: a and an.

Author: The person who wrote the words of a book.

Beginning Consonants: Consonant sounds that come at the beginning of words.

Blends: Two consonants put together to form a single sound.

Capital Letters: Letters that are used at the beginning of the names of people, places, days, months and holidays. Capital letters are also used at the beginning of sentences. These letters are sometimes called uppercase or "big" letters.

Centimeter: A measurement of length in the metric system. There are $2\frac{1}{2}$ centimeters in an inch.

Chapters: Small sections of a book.

Characters: The people or animals in a story.

Circle: A figure that is round.

Classifying: Putting things that are alike into groups.

Closed Figures: Figures whose lines connect.

Commands: Sentences that tell someone to do something.

Commutative Property: The rule in addition that states that, even if the order of the numbers is changed, the sum will be the same.

Compound Predicate: Predicate of the sentence formed by joining two verbs that have the same subject.

Compound Subject: Subject of the sentence formed by joining two nouns that have the same predicate.

Compound Words: Two words that are put together to make one new word. Example: house + boat = houseboat.

Comprehension: Understanding what you read.

Consonants: The letters b, c, d, f, g, h, j, k, l, m, n, p, q, r, s, t, v, w, x, y and z.

Consonant Blends: Two or three consonant letters in a word whose sounds combine, or blend. Examples: br, fr, gr, tr.

Consonant Teams: Two or three consonant letters that have the single sound. Examples: sh and tch.

Contractions: A short way to write two words together. Example: it is = it's.

Decimal: A number with one or more places to the right of a decimal point, such as 6.5 or 3.78. Money amounts are written with two places to the right of a decimal point, such as $1.30.

Dictionary: A reference book that gives the meaning of words and how to pronounce them.

Difference: The answer in a subtraction problem.

Digit: The symbols used to write numbers: 0, 1, 2, 3, 4, 5, 6, 7, 8 and 9.

Dime: Ten cents. It is written 10¢ or $.10.

Dollar: A dollar is equal to one hundred cents. It is written $1.00.

Double Vowel Words: When two vowels appear together in a word. Examples: tea, coat

Ending Consonants: Consonant sounds which come at the end of words.

Fact: Something that can be proven.

Fiction: A make-believe story.

Fraction: A number that names part of a whole, such as $\frac{1}{3}$ or $\frac{1}{2}$.

Geometry: Mathematics that has to do with lines and shapes.

Glossary: A little dictionary at the back of a book.

Graph: A drawing that shows information about numbers.

Guide Words: The words that appear at the top of a dictionary page to tell you what the first and the last words on that page will be.

Haiku: An Oriental form of poetry. Most have 5 syllables in the first and third lines, and 7 syllables in the middle line.

Half-Hour: Thirty minutes. It is written 0:30.

Hard and Soft c: In words where c is followed by a or u, the c usually has a hard sound (like a k). Examples: cup, cart. When c is followed by e, i or y, it usually has a soft sound (like an s). Examples: circle, fence.

Hard and Soft g: When g is followed by e, i or y, it usually has a soft sound (like j). Examples: change and gentle. The hard g sounds like the g in girl or gate.

Homophones: Words that sound the same but are spelled differently and mean different things. Example: blue and blew.

Hour: Sixty minutes. The short hand of a clock tells the hour. It is written 1:00.

Illustrator: The person who drew pictures for a book.

Inch: A unit of length in the standard measurement system.

Inference: A conclusion arrived at by what is suggested in the text.

Joining Words: Words that combine ideas in a sentence, such as "and," "but," "or" and "because."

Letter Teams: Two letters put together to make one new sound.

Long Vowels: Long vowels say their names. Examples: Long a is the sound you hear in hay. Long e is the sound you hear in me. Long i is the sound you hear in pie. Long o is the sound you hear in no. Long u is the sound you hear in cute.

Main Idea: The most important point or idea in a story.

Making Deductions: Using reasoning skills to draw conclusions.

Metric System: A system of measuring in which length is measured in millimeters, centimeters, meters and kilometers; capacity is measured in milliliters and liters; weight is measured in grams and kilograms; and temperature is measured in degrees Celsius.

Multiplication: A short way to find the sum of adding the same number a certain amount of times. For example, 7 x 4 = 28 instead of 7 + 7 + 7 + 7 = 28.

Nickel: Five cents. It is written 5¢ or $.05.

Nonfiction: A true story.

Nouns: Words that name a person, place or thing.

Open Figures: Figures whose lines do not connect.

Opinion: A feeling or belief about something that cannot be proven.

Opposites: Words that are different in every way. Example: black and white.

Ordinal Numbers: Numbers that indicate order in a series, such as first, second or third.

Pattern: Similar shapes or designs.

Penny: One cent. It is written 1¢ or $.01.

Place Value: The value of a digit, or numeral, shown by where it is in the number.

Plurals: Words that mean more than one. Examples: shoes, ladies, dishes, foxes.

Predicate: The verb in the sentence that tells the main action.

Predicting: Telling what is likely to happen, based on the facts.

Prefix: A syllable added at the beginning of a word to change its meaning. Examples: disappear, misplace.

Product: The answer of a multiplication problem.

Pronouns: Words that are used in place of nouns. "She," "he," "it" and "they" are pronouns.

Proper Nouns: The names of specific people, places and things. Proper nouns begin with a capital letter.

Quarter: Twenty-five cents. It is written 25¢ or $.25.

Questions: Sentences that ask something. A question begins with a capital letter and ends with a question mark.

R-Controlled Vowel: When r follows a vowel, it gives the vowel a different sound. Examples: her, bark, bird.

Rectangle: A figure with four corners and four sides. Sides opposite each other are the same length.

Regroup: To use ten ones to form one ten, ten tens to form 100, and so on.

Rhymes: Words that end with the same sound.

Rhyming Words: Words that sound alike at the end of a word. Example: cat and rat.

Same and Different: Being able to tell how things are the same and how they are different.

Sentences: A group of words that tells a complete idea or asks a question.

Sequencing: Putting things in the correct order, such as 7, 8, 9 or small, medium, large.

Short Vowels: Vowels that make short sounds. Examples: Short a is the sound you hear in cat. Short e is the sound you hear in leg. Short i is the sound you hear in pig. Short o is the sound in box. Short u is the sound in cup.

Silent Letters: Letters you can't hear at all, such as the gh in night, the w in wrong and the t in listen.

Simile: A figure of speech that compares two things that are alike in some way. The words "like" and "as" are used in similes. Examples: as soft as a pillow, as light as a feather.

Statements: Sentences that tell about something. Statements begin with a capital letter and end with a period.

Subtraction: Taking away or subtracting one number from another to find the difference.

Suffix: A syllable added at the end of a word to change its meaning. Examples: smaller, helpless.

Super Silent e: An e that you can't hear when it appears at the end of a word. It makes the other vowel have a long sound. Examples: cape, robe, slide.

Surprising Sentences: Sentences that tell a strong feeling. Surprising sentences begin with a capital letter and end with an exclamation point.

Syllables: The parts of words that have vowel sounds. Examples: Rab bit has two syllables. Bas ket ball has three syllables.

Synonyms: Words that mean the same or nearly the same. Example: sleepy and tired.

Table of Contents: A list at the beginning of a book, telling what is in the book and the page number.

Telling Sentences: Sentences that tell a strong feeling. Telling sentences begin with a capital letter and end with an exclamation point.

Title: The name of a book.

Tracking: Following a path.

Triangle: A figure with three corners and three sides.

Venn Diagram: A diagram that shows how two things are the same and how they are different.

Verbs: Words that tell the action in a sentence. Example: The boy ran fast.

Vowel Team: Vowels that appear together in words. Usually, the first one says its name and the second one is silent. Examples: leaf, soap, rain.

Vowels: The letters a, e, i, o, u and sometimes y.

Y as a Vowel: When y comes at the end of a word, it is a vowel. Examples: my, baby.

Alphabetical (ABC) order

Have your child alphabetize his/her word cards from the
"Spelling Concentration" game.

Have your child list all the rainforest animals (or forest or ocean
animals) that he/she can. Ask him/her to alphabetize the list on
another sheet of paper. Give him/her extra help with words that
begin with the same letter if needed.

Write the ABC's in a column down the left-hand side of a sheet
of paper. As you read a story with your child, have him/her find
and write words that begin with each letter.

Select a category. Then, help your child find a word for each
letter of the alphabet that fits that category. Example: Animals—
anteater, bear, cow, etc.

Help your child create tongue twisters using words in ABC order.
Examples: A big cat danced elegantly. Frank gave Harry icky
jellybeans.

Classifying

Have your child choose a topic and write a word list related to it. Example: Summer—hot, sun, bare feet, shorts, etc. He/she can create sentences using these words.

Help your child classify and list animals in groups: mammals, reptiles, fish, birds, amphibians, etc.

Creative Writing

Challenge your child to use his/her spelling words to create a "word find" for you to do.

Have your child make a list of rhyming words.

Have your child practice the spelling words by using all of them to create a story.

Have your child choose a topic, then write as many words as possible that fit the category. Example: volleyball: net, ball, uniform, serve, spike, bump, set, time out, sand, court, etc.

Expose your child to words with multiple meanings and have him/her look up the words in a dictionary. Have your child practice using the words in both written and spoken words.

Encourage your child to form similes with spelling words. A simile is a comparison using "like" or "as." Examples: He is as light as a feather. She is quiet like a mouse.

Help your child create a Family Book. Have your child add photos, draw pictures and write captions for an original family scrapbook.

Teach your child to write limericks. A limerick is a five-line humorous rhymed verse. Example: There once was a cat that was fat/ Who ate on a little red mat./ She said with a smile,/ "I've been here awhile,/ So you just go on now and scat!"

Create a story jar for your child. Write several tantalizing story starters on slips of paper. Some examples might be "If I found $100 . . ." or "What was that creaking sound I heard from the attic?" When your child needs a good idea for a story, he/she can draw a slip from the jar.

Dictionary Skills

Create a personal dictionary or a "Word Wall" poster for your child to keep track of each new word he/she learns.

Have a family "word of the week." Challenge family members to look up the word, to learn its spelling and to use it as much as possible during the week.

Make an alphabet book. Have your child cut big letters from magazines and glue each letter on a separate page. He/she can arrange the pages in ABC order. Then, have your child draw pictures of objects that start with each letter.

Choose a new word each day for your child to look up in the dictionary. Discuss the word's meaning. Have your child write a sentence using the new word. He/she can keep a list of the words in a word journal.

Help your child find new words on the Internet, in newspapers, on signs, etc. Have your child look them up in the dictionary. Make a collage using the words.

Following Directions

Have your child read and follow directions for constructing a model, playing a game, preparing a recipe, and so on. Ask your child to write his/her own directions for making a simple recipe or playing a simple game.

Geometry

Help your child cut out various geometric shapes and make a shape mobile to hang up.

Use construction paper to create prisms and three-dimensional objects, such as a party hat, a cube, etc.

Grammar

Have your child practice creating word families by adding "s" to the original word to make it mean more than one.

Write sentences for your child to proofread. Include both punctuation and spelling errors. Example: The bair went over the mountain?

Use your computer to write sentences for your child to correct. For example: The boys name is jim. Your child can gain valuable practice with both English skills and the computer by moving the arrow and delete keys to correct the sentence.

Graphs

Graph the birthdays of the people in your family. Ask your child questions based on the graph, such as "In which month are there the most birthdays?" "The fewest number?" "In which months are there no birthdays?"

Graph the people in your family, using criteria such as "boys," "girls," "pets," etc.

Inferences

Make riddle cards using clues for different fairy tale or cartoon characters. Play a guessing game with the cards. Let your child read the clues and name the character. Example: What little bear went hungry because a young girl ate his porridge? If you make these ahead of time, they can help pass the time on a long trip.

Put the pieces of a 12 to 20 piece puzzle in a bag. Let your child look at the pieces and make inferences about what the picture will be. Then, put the puzzle together.

Making Deductions

Put an object in a box and write clues for it. Have your child read the clues and guess what the object may be.

Measurement

Ask your child what other tools we use for measuring things (calendars and clocks to measure time, thermometer to measure temperature, etc.). Brainstorm a list of different measuring tools.

Show your child how to measure the circumference of cylindrical objects. For example, have your child predict the distance around a tree trunk. Pull a length of string around a tree trunk until the two ends meet. Cut the string. Then, measure the length of the string in inches and centimeters. Compare the actual measurement with your child's prediction.

Present a math word problem for your child to solve. Have him/her explain and write in sequence how to solve the problem.

Multiple-Meaning Words

Talk with your child about multiple-meaning words when opportunities present themselves in conversation. For example: "Did you hear the phone **ring**?" and "What a beautiful diamond **ring**!" Ask your child to brainstorm other examples of multiple-meaning words.

Parts of Speech

Play a fun "parts of speech" word game with your child. Write nouns, verbs and adjectives on index cards and have your child illustrate them. Then, let your child choose a noun card, a verb card and an adjective card and put them together to form fun sentences.

Have your child select a section of the newspaper and circle as many nouns and underline as many verbs as possible. You might ask him/her to circle plural nouns in a different color.

Patterns

Help your child find shape patterns as you drive or go for a walk together. Look for patterns in clothing, in billboards or on store signs.

Watch for word patterns as you read together. In the book *Too Much Noise* by Ann McGovern, your child can easily identify phrases that are repeated, and often, based on the story, predict the next phrase in the pattern.

Point of View

Read a chapter in a chapter book with your child. Then, ask your child to draw a picture of what happened in that chapter. You could also ask your child to draw a picture of what he/she thinks might happen next.

Read fairy tales like "The Three Little Pigs," "Cinderella," "The Three Billy Goats Gruff," "Hansel and Gretel," etc. Then, ask your child to retell the story from the point of view of the villain. Have him/her build a case explaining why the character did what he/she did.

Predicting Outcomes

While reading a story, stop periodically and have your child predict what he/she thinks will happen next.

Before reading a book with your child, ask him/her questions about the story and scan the illustrations. Ask questions beginning with who, what, why, when and how. For example: "What do you think this book is about?" "What do you think the title means?" "Who is this on the cover of the book?" "What is he/she doing?" "Do you think this is a true story or a make-believe story?"

Write an incomplete sentence using descriptive words but leave off the ending. Ask your child to finish the sentence. Example: The slinky, slimy lizard crept slowly into Marco's new, shiny bookbag and ____.

Recalling Details

Have your child choose a character from a story and write or tell about the character. Ask him/her to draw a picture of the character.

Read a fairy tale with your child. Ask him/her to tell or write the story from a different point of view. For example: Make the troll the good character in "Three Billy Goats Gruff" and the goats the bad characters.

Have your child make a story chart for a book, displaying the important events that happened at the beginning, middle and end of the story.

Your child can create a shoebox diorama displaying a scene from a favorite story, book, play, poem, and so on. A diorama is a three-dimensional scene that includes characters and objects from a story, displayed in an open box, similar to a stage. Encourage your child to be creative!

Relating to the Unknown

Choose a topic of interest to your child, such as insects, planets, sports, etc. Then, discuss what he/she knows and what he/she wants to learn about the topic. Formulate questions that will help your child learn new information based upon past knowledge. Example: How does a bee protect itself?

Retell

Read a book together. Then, ask your child to retell the story emphasizing what happened in the beginning, middle and end.

Rhymes

Make up silly sentences with your child to practice rhyming skills. For example, "I saw a paper star when I cleaned out the ___." You may also want to say a series of words and have your child tell you which one doesn't rhyme: coat, float, dish, goat.

Same and Different

Choose two animals, sports, toys, TV programs, etc. and ask your child to tell you how they are the same or how they are different.

Have your child compare three rooms in your home. Ask him/her to tell you how they are the same and how they are different.

Sentences

Create word or sentence "dot-to-dots." Instead of numbers, write letters or words. Have your child connect the dots in the correct sequence to write a word or to correctly order a sentence.

Play a game which helps your child learn to use words in context. Write several words on index cards. Take turns drawing a card and using the word on the card in a sentence.

Print sentences or copy a story on a sheet of paper. Leave blanks for key words. Have your child read the story and supply the missing words.

Write descriptive sentences on long cardboard strips. Have your child read the sentences. Then, cut the sentences into word sections and have your child put the sentences back in order.

Sequencing

Invite your child to recreate a story as a comic strip. List six or more important events or scenes from a story in sequence. Then, have your child write each event on a separate sheet of paper and draw an accompanying picture. Glue the pages in order on large sheets of colorful construction paper.

Write or tell a story together. Begin the story. After a few sentences, have your child continue the story. Take turns until you get to the end.

Use the comics to help your child practice sequence. Select comics that show a simple sequence, and read the comic strip with your child. Cut the comic strip apart, and challenge your child to rearrange it in the correct order. You could also draw simple pictures in a series, and have your child draw a picture to show what would happen next. Pictures from the family photo album are also fun to sequence. Your child can use the visual clues of growth to help arrange them in sequential order.

Spelling

Create a deck of cards with letters and letter teams. Have your child try to make words from the cards drawn.

Write each of your child's spelling words on an index card. Cut apart the cards at the syllables. Mix up the cards and have your child try to put the original words back together.

Play "Spell-o" with your child. Write each word in a box on a 5 x 5 grid. As you name a spelling word, have your child spell it back to you. He/she can then cover the square. When the card has five in a row covered, your child has "Spell-o!"

Fill a squirt bottle with water and let your child spell words by squirting water on dry pavement.

Challenge your child to think of as many words as possible with letter teams such as oy. Try other letter teams such as au, aw, ee and ow. Allow your child to check a dictionary if he/she needs to.

Synonyms, Antonyms, Homophones

Encourage your child to create more varied and interesting sentences by substituting synonyms for words he/she uses repeatedly. As your child reads his/her writing to you, point out places where a synonym might be used, such as the use of the words "tiny" or "small" instead of "little."

Teach your child how to use a thesaurus to find synonyms (words that have almost the same meaning) of each spelling word. A thesaurus organized like a dictionary is the easiest to use.

Make a synonym memory game with your child. Write ten words on index cards. Then, write synonyms for the words on additional index cards. Mix up the cards and place them facedown to play. Let your child turn over two cards at a time. If he/she matches two words which are synonyms, he/she gets to keep the cards. If the two words do not match, he/she must return the cards to their position. Then, the next player takes his/her turn. Play continues until all of the cards are gone. This game may also be played with words and their antonyms.

Act out a word (hello) from your list of antonyms and ask your child to act out the antonym (goodbye).

Create a list of antonyms or homophones with your child. Then, ask your child to write a poem or limerick using the words.

Using the list of homophones, ask your child to write and illustrate sentences using a pair of homophones. Examples: I have a pair of pears. The bear had bare feet.

Time

Help your child create a paper plate clock. Use a paper fastener to attach the minute and hour hands. Suggest different hour and half-hour times for your child to show on the clock face.

Tracking

Draw a map of your home or neighborhood. Have your child draw paths from your home to other places in the area. Go for a walk or a drive, following one of the paths your child drew.

Have your child write, in order, how to escape from your home in case of an emergency. Then, follow the path with your family.

Visualizing

Ask your child to form a picture of a memory in his/her mind. Then, ask him/her to write or draw a description of what he/she sees.

Cut out pictures of scenery from old magazines. Share the pictures with your child. Ask him/her to tell you what images come to mind as he/she views them.

6 — All About Me!

Directions: Fill in the blanks to tell all about you!

Name __Answers will vary__
    (First)   (Last)
Address _____
City _____ State _____
Phone number _____
Age _____

Places I have visited: __Answers will vary__
_____
_____
_____

My favorite hobbies: __Answers will vary__
_____
_____
_____

7 — Let's Begin: b, c, d, f, g, h, j

Directions: Fill in the beginning consonant for each word.

Example: _c_ at

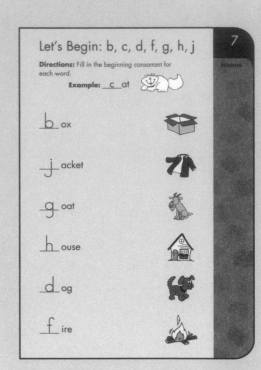

__b__ ox

__j__ acket

__g__ oat

__h__ ouse

__d__ og

__f__ ire

8 — Let's Begin: k, l, m, n, p, q, r

Directions: Write the letter that makes the beginning sound for each picture.

__m__   __q__   __r__

__n__   __m__   __l__

__k__   __r__   __q__

__p__   __n__   __m__

9 — Let's Begin: s, t, v, w, x, y, z

Directions: Write the letter under each picture that makes the beginning sound.

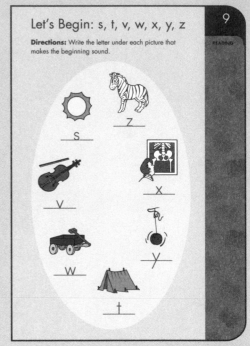

__s__   __z__

__v__   __x__

__w__   __y__

__t__

10 — Last Letters: b, d, f, g

Directions: Fill in the ending consonant for each word.

ma __n__

cu __b__

roo __f__

do __g__

be __d__

bi __b__

11 — Last Letters: k, l, m, n, p, r

Directions: Fill in the ending consonant for each word.

nai __l__

ca __n__

gu __m__

ca __r__

truc __k__

ca __p__

pai __l__

12 — Last Letters: s, t, x

Directions: Fill in the ending consonant for each word.

ca __t__

bo __x__

bu __s__

fo __x__

boa __t__

ma __t__

13 — Bring on the Blends!

Consonant blends are two or three consonant letters in a word whose sounds combine, or blend. **Examples: br, fr, gr, pr, tr**

Directions: Look at each picture. Say its name. Write the blend you hear at the beginning of each word.

__tr__   __fr__   __br__

__pr__   __tr__   __gr__

__fr__   __gr__   __br__

__tr__   __pr__   __tr__

14 — Blends: fl, br, pl, sk, sn

Blends are two consonants put together to form a single sound.

Directions: Look at the pictures and say their names. Write the letters for the beginning sound in each word.

__br__   __sk__

__fl__   __br__

__fl__   __sn__

__br__   __pl__

__sn__   __fl__

15 — Blends: bl, sl, cr, cl

Directions: Look at the pictures and say their names. Write the letters for the beginning sound in each word.

__cl__ own   __bl__ anket   __cr__ ayon

__cl__ ock   __sl__ ide   __cl__ oud

__sl__ ed   __cr__ ab   __cr__ ocodile

16 — Tell Me a Riddle

Directions: Write a word from the word box to answer each riddle.

| clock | blow | climb | slipper |
| gloves | clap | blocks | flashlight |

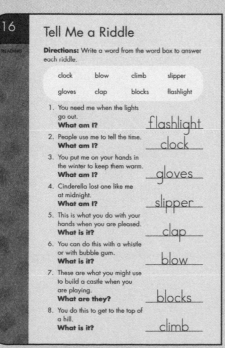

1. You need me when the lights go out.
   What am I? __flashlight__

2. People use me to tell the time.
   What am I? __clock__

3. You put me on your hands in the winter to keep them warm.
   What am I? __gloves__

4. Cinderella lost one like me at midnight.
   What am I? __slipper__

5. This is what you do with your hands when you are pleased.
   What is it? __clap__

6. You can do this with a whistle or with bubble gum.
   What is it? __blow__

7. These are what you might use to build a castle when you are playing.
   What are they? __blocks__

8. You do this to get to the top of a hill.
   What is it? __climb__

17 — Teammates

Consonant teams are two or three consonant letters that have a single sound. **Examples: sh and tch**

Directions: Write each word from the word box next to its picture. Underline the consonant team in each word. Circle the consonant team in each word in the box.

| ben(ch) | ma(tch) | (sh)oe | (th)imble | (sh)ell |
| pea(ch) | wa(tch) | (wh)ale | (ch)air | (wh)eel |

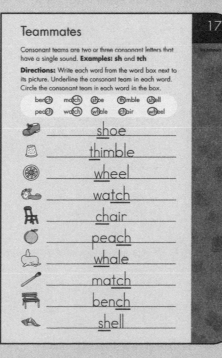

__shoe__

__thimble__

__wheel__

__watch__

__chair__

__peach__

__whale__

__match__

__bench__

__shell__

226

ANSWER KEY

18

Join the Team

Directions: Look at the first picture in each row. Circle the pictures that have the same sound.

whistle

shoe

chin

thumb

19

Sort It Out

Directions: Look at the words in the word box. Write all of the words that end with the **ng** sound in the column under the picture of the **ring**. Write all of the words that end with the **nk** sound under the picture of the **sink**. Finish the sentences with words from the word box.

strong rank bring bank honk hang thank
long hunk song stung bunk sang junk

ng	nk
strong	rank
long	hunk
bring	bank
song	honk
stung	bunk
hang	thank
sang	junk

1. <u>Honk</u> your horn when you get to my house.
2. He was <u>stung</u> by a bumblebee.
3. We are going to put our money in a <u>bank</u>.
4. I want to <u>thank</u> you for the birthday present.
5. My brother and I sleep in <u>bunk</u> beds.

20

Shhh! Silent Letters

Some words have letters you can't hear at all, such as the **gh** in **night**, the **w** in **wrong**, the **l** in **walk**, the **k** in **knee**, the **b** in **climb** and the **t** in **listen**.

Directions: Look at the words in the word box. Write the word under its picture. Underline the silent letters.

knife light calf wrench lamb eight
wrist whistle comb thumb knob knee

eight   wrist   knee

calf   lamb   knob

whistle   light   wrench

comb   thumb   knife

21

Review

Directions: Read the story. Circle the consonant teams (two or three letters) and silent letters in the underlined words. Be sure to check for more than one team in a word! One has been done for you.

One day last Spring my family went on a picnic. My father picked out a pretty spot next to a stream. While my brother and I climbed a tree, my mother spread out a sheet and placed the food on it. But before we could eat, a skunk walked out of the woods! Mother screamed and scared the skunk. It sprayed us with a terrible smell! Now, we think it is a funny story. But that day, we ran!

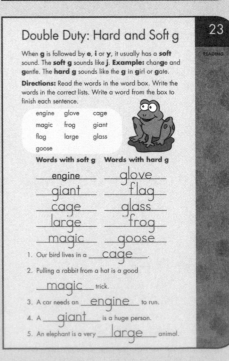

Directions: Write the words with three-letter blends on the lines.

Spring
stream
spread
screamed
sprayed

22

Double Duty: Hard and Soft c

When **c** is followed by **e**, **i** or **y**, it usually has a **soft** sound. The **soft c** sounds like **s**. For example, **c**ircle and fen**c**e. When **c** is followed by **a** or **u**, it usually has a **hard** sound. The **hard c** sounds like **k**. For example, **c**up and **c**art.

Directions: Read the words in the word box. Write the words in the correct lists. One word will be in both. Write a word from the box to finish each sentence.

pencil cookie dance popcorn cent
circus lucky mice tractor card

Words with soft c	Words with hard c
pencil	circus
dance	popcorn
cent	lucky
mice	tractor
circus	cookie
	card

1. Another word for a penny is a <u>cent</u>.
2. A cat likes to chase <u>mice</u>.
3. You will see animals and clowns at the <u>circus</u>.
4. Will you please sharpen my <u>pencil</u>?

23

Double Duty: Hard and Soft g

When **g** is followed by **e**, **i** or **y**, it usually has a **soft** sound. The **soft g** sounds like **j**. **Example:** chan**g**e and **g**entle. The **hard g** sounds like the **g** in **g**irl or **g**ate.

Directions: Read the words in the word box. Write the words in the correct lists. Write a word from the box to finish each sentence.

engine glove cage
magic frog giant
flag large glass
goose

Words with soft g	Words with hard g
engine	glove
giant	flag
cage	glass
large	frog
magic	goose

1. Our bird lives in a <u>cage</u>.
2. Pulling a rabbit from a hat is a good <u>magic</u> trick.
3. A car needs an <u>engine</u> to run.
4. A <u>giant</u> is a huge person.
5. An elephant is a very <u>large</u> animal.

24 Letter Detector: Short Vowels

Vowels can make **short** or **long** sounds. The **short a** sounds like the **a** in c**a**t. The **short e** is like the **e** in l**e**g. The **short i** sounds like the **i** in p**i**g. The **short o** sounds like the **o** in b**o**x. The **short u** sounds like the **u** in c**u**p.

Directions: Look at each picture. Write the missing short vowel letter.

p_u_p   n_e_t   s_o_ck

_a_x   l_i_ps   h_a_t

f_o_x   t_e_nt   p_i_n

25 Super Silent e

Long vowel sounds have the same sound as their names. When a **Super Silent e** appears at the end of a word, you can't hear it, but it makes the other vowel have a long sound. For example: **tub** has a **short** vowel sound, and **tube** has a **long** vowel sound.

Directions: Look at the following pictures. Decide if the word has a short or long vowel sound. Circle the correct word. Watch for the **Super Silent e**!

can (cane)   tub tube   rob (robe)

pin pine   (cap) cape   not (note)

slid (slide)   dim (dime)   tap (tape)

26 Letter Detector: Long Vowels

Directions: Say the name of the pictures. Listen for the long vowel sounds. Write the missing long vowel sound under each picture.

c_a_ke   h_i_ke   n_o_se

_a_pe   c_u_be   gr_a_pe

r_a_ke   b_o_ne   k_i_te

27 Review

Directions: Read the words in each box. Cross out the word that does not belong.

long vowels	short vowels
cube	man
~~cup~~	pet
rake	fix
me	~~ice~~

long vowels	short vowels
soap	cat
seed	pin
read	~~rain~~
~~mat~~	frog

Directions: Write **short** or **long** to label the words in each box.

long vowels	short vowels
hose	hose
take	take
bead	bead
cube	cube
eat	eat
see	see

28 R in Charge

When a vowel is followed by the letter **r**, it has a different sound.

Example: he and **her**

Directions: Write a word from the word box to finish each sentence. Notice the sound of the vowel followed by an **r**.

park   chair   horse   bark   bird
hurt   girl   hair   store   ears

1. A dog likes to _bark_
2. You buy food at a _store_.
3. Children like to play at the _park_.
4. An animal you can ride is a _horse_.
5. You hear with your _ears_.
6. A robin is a kind of _bird_.
7. If you fall down, you might get _hurt_.
8. The opposite of a boy is a _girl_.
9. You comb and brush your _hair_.
10. You sit down on a _chair_.

29 Double Trouble

Usually when two vowels appear together, the first one says its name and the second one is silent.

Example: bean

Directions: Unscramble the double vowel words below. Write the correct word on the line.

ocat _coat_

mtea _meat_

teas _seat_

ogat _goat_

atli _tail_

etar _tear_

eetf _feet_

otab _boat_

spea _peas_

apil _pail_

30 — Team Time: ou, ow, au, aw

The vowel teams **ou** and **ow** can have the same sound. You can hear it in the words **clown** and **cloud**. The vowel teams **au** and **aw** have the same sound. You hear it in the words **because** and **law**.

Directions: Look at the pictures. Write the correct vowel team to complete the words. The first one is done for you. You may need to use a dictionary to help you with the correct spelling.

_au_ to   cl_OW_n   h_OU_se

fl_OW_er   s_aw_   _OW_l

p_OW_der   m_OU_th   j_aw_

31 — Team Time: ea

The vowel team **ea** can have a **short e** sound like in **head**, or a **long e** sound like in **bead**. An **ea** followed by an **r** makes a sound like the one in **ear** or like the one in **heard**.

Directions: Read the story. Listen for the sound **ea** makes in the bold words.

Have you ever **read** a book or **heard** a story about a **bear**? You might have **learned** that bears sleep through the winter. Some bears may sleep the whole **season**. Sometimes they look almost **dead**! But they are very much alive. As the cold winter passes and the spring **weather** comes **near**, they wake up. After such a nice rest, they must be **ready** to **eat** a **really** big **meal**!

words with long ea

season
eat
really
meal

words with short ea

read
dead
weather
ready

ea followed by r

heard
bear
learned
near

32 — Team Time: ie, ei, eigh, ey

The vowel team **ie** makes the **long e** sound like in **believe**. The team **ei** also makes the **long e** sound like in **either**. But **ei** can also make a **long a** sound like in **eight**.

Directions: Circle the **ei** words with the **long a** sound.

(neighbor)   (veil)   receive
(reindeer)   (reign)   ceiling

The teams **eigh** and **ey** also make the **long a** sound.

Directions: Finish the sentences with words from the word box.

obey   weigh   thief   field   ceiling

1. Rules are for us to _____obey_____.
2. The bird got out of its cage and flew up to the _____ceiling_____.
3. How much do you _____weigh_____?
4. They caught the _____thief_____ who took my bike.
5. Corn grows in a _____field_____.

33 — Team Time: oi, oy, ou, ow

Directions: Look at the first picture in each row. Circle the pictures that have the same sound.

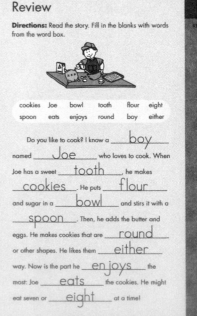

oi — oil

oy — toy

ou — couch

ow — howl

34 — Team Time: ai, ee

Directions: Write in the vowel team **ai** or **ee** to complete each word.

r_ai_n   f_ee_d

s_ee_d   p_ai_l

s_ai_l   cr_ee_k

35 — Review

Directions: Read the story. Fill in the blanks with words from the word box.

cookies   Joe   bowl   tooth   flour   eight
spoon   eats   enjoys   round   boy   either

Do you like to cook? I know a _____boy_____ named _____Joe_____ who loves to cook. When Joe has a sweet _____tooth_____, he makes _____cookies_____. He puts _____flour_____ and sugar in a _____bowl_____ and stirs it with a _____spoon_____. Then, he adds the butter and eggs. He makes cookies that are _____round_____ or other shapes. He likes them _____either_____ way. Now is the part he _____enjoys_____ the most: Joe _____eats_____ the cookies. He might eat seven or _____eight_____ at a time!

36 — That's Y!

When **y** comes at the end of a word, it is a vowel. When **y** is the only vowel at the end of a one-syllable word, it has the sound of a **long i** (like in **my**). When **y** is the only vowel at the end of a word with more than one syllable, it has the sound of a **long e** (like in **baby**).

Directions: Look at the words in the word box. If the word has the sound of a **long i**, write it under the word **my**. If the word has the sound of a **long e**, write it under the word **baby**. Write the word from the word box that answers each riddle.

happy   penny   fry   try   dry
bunny   windy   sky   party   fly

my	baby
fry	happy
try	bunny
sky	penny
dry	windy
fly	party

1. It takes five of these to make a nickel. **penny**
2. This is what you call a baby rabbit. **bunny**
3. It is often blue and you can see it if you look up. **sky**
4. You might have one of these on your birthday. **party**

37 — Putting It Together

Compound words are two words that are put together to make one new word.

Directions: Read the sentences. Fill in the blank with a compound word from the box.

raincoat   bedroom   lunchbox   hallway   sandbox

1. A box with sand is a **sandbox**
2. The way through a hall is a **hallway**
3. A box for lunch is a **lunchbox**
4. A coat for the rain is a **raincoat**
5. A room with a bed is a **bedroom**

38 — What's Cooking?

Compound words are formed by putting together two smaller words.

Directions: Help the cook brew her stew. Mix words from the first column with words from the second column to make new words. Write your new words on the lines at the bottom.

grand	brows
snow	light
eye	stairs
down	string
rose	book
shoe	mother
note	ball
moon	bud

1. grandmother
2. snowball
3. eyebrows
4. downstairs
5. rosebud
6. shoestring
7. notebook
8. moonlight

39 — Two-for-One Special

Directions: Draw a line under the compound word in each sentence. On the line, write the two words that make up the compound word.

1. A <u>firetruck</u> came to help put out the fire. **fire   truck**
2. I will be nine years old on my next <u>birthday</u>. **birth   day**
3. We built a <u>treehouse</u> at the back. **tree   house**
4. Dad put a <u>scarecrow</u> in his garden. **scare   crow**
5. It is fun to make <u>footprints</u> in the snow. **foot   prints**
6. I like to read the comics in the <u>newspaper</u>. **news   paper**
7. <u>Cowboys</u> ride horses and use lassos. **cow   boys**

40 — Short and Sweet

Contractions are a short way to write two words, such as **isn't**, **I've** and **weren't**. **Example: it is = it's**

Directions: Draw a line from each word pair to its contraction.

I am — I'm
it is — it's
you are — you're
we are — we're
they are — they're
she is — she's
he is — he's

41 — We Love Contractions!

Directions: Cut out the two words and put them together to show what two words make the contraction. Glue them over the contraction.

can not   I will   he is
I am   will not   we have

-----
cut out

Put Your Hands Together · 43

Words are made up of parts called **syllables**. Each syllable has a vowel sound. One way to count syllables is to clap as you say the word.

Example:
cat	1 clap	1 syllable
table	2 claps	2 syllables
butterfly	3 claps	3 syllables

Directions: "Clap out" the words below. Write how many syllables each word has.

movie	2
piano	3
tree	1
bicycle	3
sun	1
cabinet	3
football	2
dog	1
basket	2
swimmer	2
rainbow	2
paper	2
picture	2

Give Me a Break · 44

Dividing a word into syllables can help you read a new word. You also might divide syllables when you are writing if you run out of space on a line. Many words contain two consonants that are next to each other. A word can usually be divided between two consonants.

Directions: Divide each word into two syllables. The first one is done for you.

kitten	kit ten
lumber	lum ber
batter	bat ter
winter	win ter
funny	fun ny
harder	hard er
dirty	dir ty
sister	sis ter

Break it Up! · 45

When a double consonant is used in the middle of a word, the word can usually be divided between the consonants.

Directions: Look at the words in the word box. Divide each word into two syllables. Leave space between each syllable. One is done for you.

butter	puppy	kitten	yellow
dinner	chatter	ladder	happy
pillow	letter	mitten	summer

but ter	chat ter	mit ten
din ner	let ter	yel low
pil low	kit ten	hap py
pup py	lad der	sum mer

Many words are divided between two consonants that are not alike.

Directions: Look at the words in the word box. Divide each word into two syllables. One is done for you.

window	doctor	number
mister	winter	pencil
barber	sister	picture

win dow	doc tor	num ber
mis ter	win ter	pen cil
bar ber	sis ter	pic ture

Add It On · 46

A **suffix** is a syllable that is added at the end of a word to change its meaning.

Directions: Add the suffixes to the root words to make new words. Use your new words to complete the sentences.

help + ful =	helpful
care + less =	careless
talk + ed =	talked
love + ly =	lovely
loud + er =	louder

1. My mother __talked__ to my teacher about my homework.
2. The radio was __louder__ than the television.
3. Sally is always __helpful__ to her mother.
4. The flowers are __lovely__.
5. It is __careless__ to cross the street without looking both ways.

Backward Nan · 47

Directions: Read the story. Underline the words that end with **est**, **ed** or **ing**. On the lines below, write the root words for each word you underlined.

The funniest book I ever read was about a girl named Nan. Nan did everything backward. She even spelled her name backward. Nan slept in the day and played at night. She dried her hair before washing it. She turned on the light after she finished her book—which she read from the back to the front! When it rained, Nan waited until she was inside before opening her umbrella. She even walked backward. The silliest part: The only thing Nan did forward was back up!

1.	funny	8.	finish
2.	name	9.	rain
3.	spell	10.	wait
4.	play	11.	open
5.	dry	12.	walk
6.	wash	13.	silly
7.	turn		

The Three Rs · 48

Prefixes are syllables added to the beginning of words that change their meaning. The prefix **re** means "again."

Directions: Read the story. Then, follow the instructions.

Kim wants to find ways she can save the Earth. She studies the "three R's"—reduce, reuse and recycle. Reduce means to make less. Both reuse and recycle mean to use again.

Add **re** to the beginning of each word below. Use the new words to complete the sentences.

re build	re fill
re read	re tell
re write	re run

1. The race was a tie, so Dawn and Kathy had to __rerun__ it.
2. The block wall fell down, so Simon had to __rebuild__ it.
3. The water bottle was empty, so Luna had to __refill__ it.
4. Javier wrote a good story, but he wanted to __rewrite__ it to make it better.
5. The teacher told a story, and students had to __retell__ it.
6. Toni didn't understand the directions, so she had to __reread__ them.

Prefix Power
49 READING

Directions: Change the meaning of the sentences by adding the prefixes to the **bold** words.

The boy was **lucky** because he guessed the answer **correctly**.

The boy was (un) __unlucky__ because he guessed the answer (in) __incorrectly__.

When Mary **behaved**, she felt **happy**.

When Mary (mis) __misbehaved__, she felt (un) __unhappy__.

Mike wore his jacket **buttoned** because the dance was **formal**.

Mike wore his jacket (un) __unbuttoned__ because the dance was (in) __informal__.

Tim **understood** because he was **familiar** with the book.

Tim (mis) __misunderstood__ because he was (un) __unfamiliar__ with the book.

Review
50 READING

Directions: Read each sentence. Look at the words in **bold**. Circle the prefix and write the root word on the line.

1. The (pre)**view** of the movie was funny.
   __view__
2. We always drink (non)**fat** milk.
   __fat__
3. We will have to (re)**schedule** the trip.
   __schedule__
4. Are you tired of (re)**runs** on television?
   __run__
5. I have (out)**grown** my new shoes already.
   __grow__
6. You must have (mis)**placed** the papers.
   __place__
7. Police (en)**force** the laws of the city.
   __force__
8. I (dis)**liked** that book.
   __like__
9. The boy (dis)**trusted** the big dog.
   __trust__
10. Try to (en)**joy** yourself at the party.
    __joy__

Mike's Bike
51 READING

Directions: Read the story about bike safety. Answer the questions below the story.

Mike has a red bike. He likes his bike. Mike wears a helmet. Mike wears knee pads and elbow pads. They keep him safe. Mike stops at signs. Mike looks both ways. Mike is safe on his bike.

1. What color is Mike's bike? __red__

2. Which sentence in the story tells why Mike wears pads and a helmet? Write it here.
   __They keep him safe.__

3. What else does Mike do to keep safe?
   He __stops__ at signs and __looks__ both ways.

Total Recall
52 READING

Directions: Read about Nikki's pets. Then, answer the questions.

Nikki has two cats, Tiger and Sniffer, and two dogs, Spot and Wiggles. Tiger is an orange striped cat who likes to sleep under a big tree and pretend she is a real tiger. Sniffer is a gray cat who likes to sniff the flowers in Nikki's garden. Spot is a Dalmatian with many black spots. Wiggles is a big furry brown dog who wiggles all over when he is happy.

1. Which dog is brown and furry? __Wiggles__
2. What color is Tiger? __orange with stripes__
3. What kind of dog is Spot? __Dalmation__
4. Which cat likes to sniff flowers? __Sniffer__
5. Where does Tiger like to sleep? __under a big tree__
6. Who wiggles all over when he is happy?
   __Wiggles__

People on the Go
53 READING

Directions: Read the story about different kinds of transportation. Answer the questions with words from the story.

People use many kinds of transportation. Boats float on the water. Some people fish in a boat. Airplanes fly in the sky. Flying in a plane is a fast way to get somewhere. Trains run on a track. The first car is the engine. The last car is the caboose. Some people even sleep in beds on a train! A car has four wheels. Most people have a car. A car rides on roads. A bus can hold many people. A bus rides on roads. Most children ride a bus to school.

1. A boat floats on the __water__.
2. If you want to get somewhere fast, which transportation would you use?
   __airplane__
3. The first car on a train is called an engine and the last car is a __caboose__.
4. __Children__ ride on a bus.
5. A __car__ has four wheels.

Dairy Delights
54 READING

Directions: Read the story. Answer the questions. Try the recipe.

Cows Give Us Milk

Cows live on a farm. The farmer milks the cows to get the milk. Many things are made from milk. We make ice cream, sour cream, cottage cheese and butter from milk. Butter is fun to make! You can learn to make your own butter. First, you need cream. Put the cream in a jar and shake it. Then, you need to pour off the liquid. Next, you put the butter in a bowl. Add a little salt and stir! Finally, spread it on crackers and eat!

1. What animal gives us milk? __cow__
2. What 4 things are made from milk?
   __ice cream__ __cottage cheese__
   __sour cream__ __butter__
3. What did the story teach you to make? __butter__
4. Put the steps in order. Place 1, 2, 3, 4 by the sentence.
   __4__ Spread the butter on crackers and eat!
   __2__ Shake cream in a jar.
   __1__ Start with cream.
   __3__ Add salt to the butter.

Get the Story Straight   55

Spencer likes to make new friends. Today, he made friends with the dog in the picture.

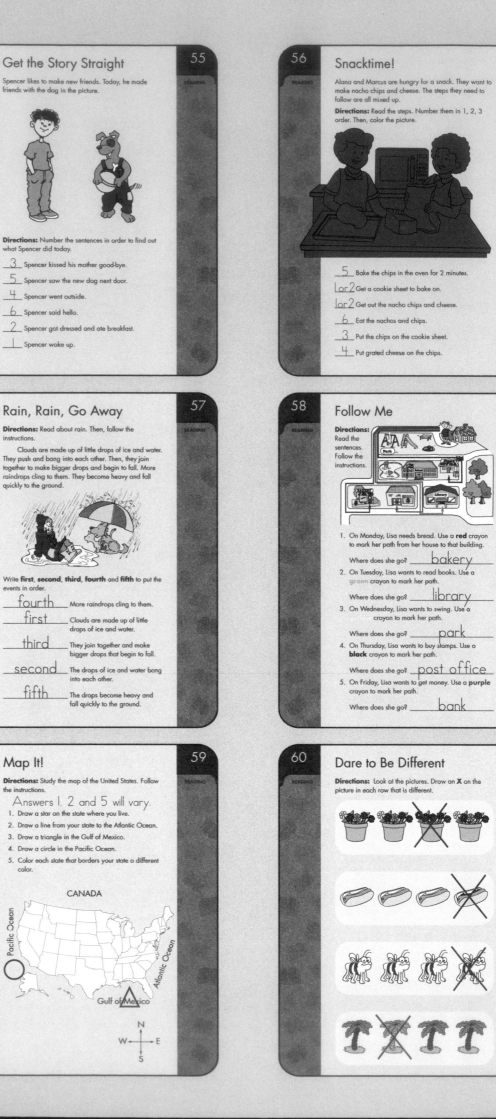

Directions: Number the sentences in order to find out what Spencer did today.

_3_ Spencer kissed his mother good-bye.

_5_ Spencer saw the new dog next door.

_4_ Spencer went outside.

_6_ Spencer said hello.

_2_ Spencer got dressed and ate breakfast.

_1_ Spencer woke up.

Snacktime!   56

Alana and Marcus are hungry for a snack. They want to make nacho chips and cheese. The steps they need to follow are all mixed up.

Directions: Read the steps. Number them in 1, 2, 3 order. Then, color the picture.

_5_ Bake the chips in the oven for 2 minutes.

_1 or 2_ Get a cookie sheet to bake on.

_1 or 2_ Get out the nacho chips and cheese.

_6_ Eat the nachos and chips.

_3_ Put the chips on the cookie sheet.

_4_ Put grated cheese on the chips.

Rain, Rain, Go Away   57

Directions: Read about rain. Then, follow the instructions.

Clouds are made up of little drops of ice and water. They push and bang into each other. Then, they join together to make bigger drops and begin to fall. More raindrops cling to them. They become heavy and fall quickly to the ground.

Write **first, second, third, fourth** and **fifth** to put the events in order.

fourth More raindrops cling to them.

first Clouds are made up of little drops of ice and water.

third They join together and make bigger drops that begin to fall.

second The drops of ice and water bang into each other.

fifth The drops become heavy and fall quickly to the ground.

Follow Me   58

Directions: Read the sentences. Follow the instructions.

1. On Monday, Lisa needs bread. Use a **red** crayon to mark her path from her house to that building.

   Where does she go? _bakery_

2. On Tuesday, Lisa wants to read books. Use a **green** crayon to mark her path.

   Where does she go? _library_

3. On Wednesday, Lisa wants to swing. Use a **yellow** crayon to mark her path.

   Where does she go? _park_

4. On Thursday, Lisa wants to buy stamps. Use a **black** crayon to mark her path.

   Where does she go? _post office_

5. On Friday, Lisa wants to get money. Use a **purple** crayon to mark her path.

   Where does she go? _bank_

Map It!   59

Directions: Study the map of the United States. Follow the instructions.

Answers 1, 2 and 5 will vary.

1. Draw a star on the state where you live.
2. Draw a line from your state to the Atlantic Ocean.
3. Draw a triangle in the Gulf of Mexico.
4. Draw a circle in the Pacific Ocean.
5. Color each state that borders your state a different color.

CANADA

Pacific Ocean

Atlantic Ocean

Gulf of Mexico

N
W · E
S

Dare to Be Different   60

Directions: Look at the pictures. Draw an **X** on the picture in each row that is different.

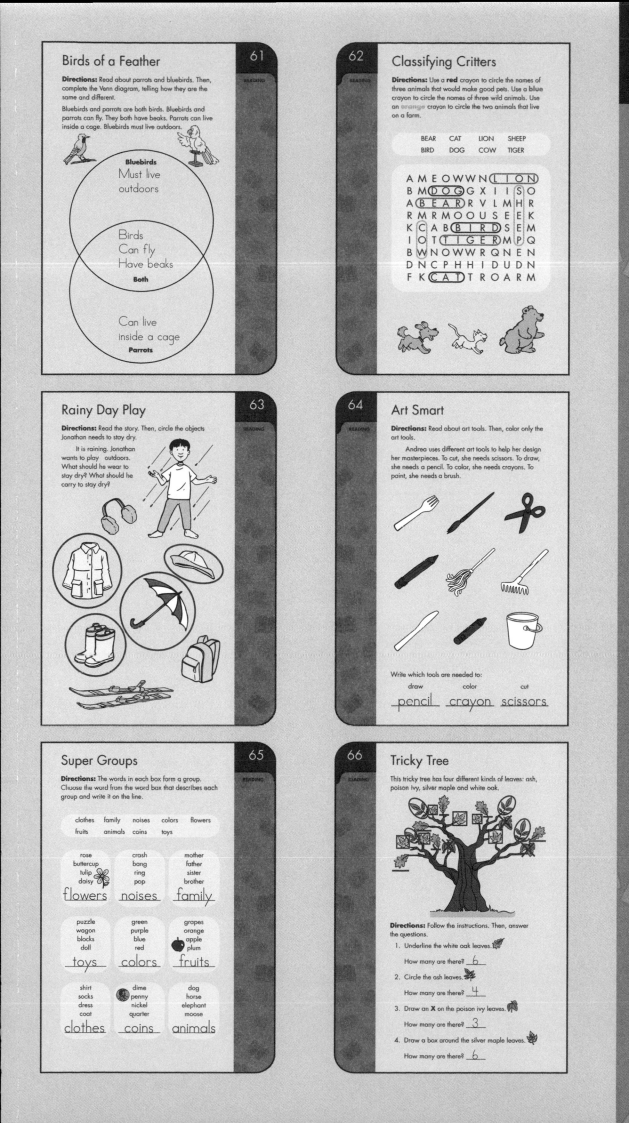

Birds of a Feather 61

Directions: Read about parrots and bluebirds. Then, complete the Venn diagram, telling how they are the same and different.

Bluebirds and parrots are both birds. Bluebirds and parrots can fly. They both have beaks. Parrots can live inside a cage. Bluebirds must live outdoors.

Bluebirds
Must live outdoors

Birds
Can fly
Have beaks
Both

Can live inside a cage
Parrots

62 Classifying Critters

Directions: Use a **red** crayon to circle the names of three animals that would make good pets. Use a **blue** crayon to circle the names of three wild animals. Use an orange crayon to circle the two animals that live on a farm.

BEAR	CAT	LION	SHEEP
BIRD	DOG	COW	TIGER

A M E O W W N (L I O N)
B M (D O G) G X I I S O
A (B E A R) R V L M H R
R M R M O O U S E E K
K C A B (B I R D S) E M
I O T (T I G E R) M P Q
B W N O W W R Q N E N
D N C P H H I D U D N
F K (C A T) T R O A R M

Rainy Day Play 63

Directions: Read the story. Then, circle the objects Jonathan needs to stay dry.

It is raining. Jonathan wants to play outdoors. What should he wear to stay dry? What should he carry to stay dry?

64 Art Smart

Directions: Read about art tools. Then, color only the art tools.

Andrea uses different art tools to help her design her masterpieces. To cut, she needs scissors. To draw, she needs a pencil. To color, she needs crayons. To paint, she needs a brush.

Write which tools are needed to:

draw	color	cut
pencil	crayon	scissors

Super Groups 65

Directions: The words in each box form a group. Choose the word from the word box that describes each group and write it on the line.

clothes   family   noises   colors   flowers
fruits   animals   coins   toys

rose buttercup tulip daisy	crash bang ring pop	mother father sister brother
flowers	**noises**	**family**

puzzle wagon blocks doll	green purple blue red	grapes orange apple plum
toys	**colors**	**fruits**

shirt socks dress coat	dime penny nickel quarter	dog horse elephant moose
clothes	**coins**	**animals**

66 Tricky Tree

This tricky tree has four different kinds of leaves: ash, poison ivy, silver maple and white oak.

Directions: Follow the instructions. Then, answer the questions.

1. Underline the white oak leaves.
   How many are there? 6

2. Circle the ash leaves.
   How many are there? 4

3. Draw an **X** on the poison ivy leaves.
   How many are there? 3

4. Draw a box around the silver maple leaves.
   How many are there? 6

A Look at Ladybugs

Directions: Read about ladybugs. Then, answer the questions.

Have you ever seen a ladybug? Ladybugs are red. They have black spots. They have six legs. Ladybugs are pretty!

1. What color are ladybugs? __red__
2. What color are their spots? __black__
3. How many legs do ladybugs have? __six__

67

Paper Puppets

Directions: Read about paper-bag puppets. Then, follow the instructions.

It is easy to make a hand puppet. You need a small paper bag. You need colored paper. You need glue. You need scissors. Are you ready?

1. Circle the main idea:
   You need scissors.
   (Making a hand puppet is easy.)
2. Write the four objects you need to make a paper-bag puppet.
   1) __small paper bag__
   2) __colored paper__
   3) __glue__
   4) __scissors__
3. Draw a face on the paper-bag puppet.

68

Nice to Meet You

Directions: Read about how to meet a dog. Then, follow the instructions.

Do not try to pet a dog right away. First, let the dog sniff your hand. Do not move quickly. Do not talk loudly. Just let the dog sniff.

1. Predict what the dog will let you do if it likes you.
   __Pet it.__
2. What should you let the dog do?
   __Sniff your hand.__
3. Name three things you should not do when you meet a dog.
   1) __try to pet it__
   2) __move quickly__
   3) __talk loudly__

69

Sean Leads the Team

Directions: Read about Sean's basketball game. Then, answer the questions.

Sean really likes to play basketball. One sunny day, he decided to ask his friends to play basketball at the park, but there were six people—Sean, Aki, Lance, Kate, Zac and Oralia. A basketball team only allows five to play at a time. So, Sean decided to be the coach. Sean and his friends had fun.

1. How many kids wanted to play basketball? __six__
2. Write their names in ABC order:
   __Aki__
   __Kate__
   __Lance__
   __Oralia__
   __Sean__
   __Zac__
3. How many players can play on a basketball team at a time? __five__
4. Where did they play basketball? __at the park__
5. Who decided to be the coach? __Sean__

70

Rained Out

Predicting is telling what is likely to happen based on the facts.

Directions: Read the story. Then, check each sentence below that tells how the story could end.

One cloudy day, Juan and his baseball team, the Bears, played the Crocodiles. It was the last half of the fifth inning, and it started to rain. The coaches and umpires had to decide what to do.

✓ They kept playing until nine innings were finished.

✓ They ran for cover and waited until the rain stopped.

___ Each player grabbed an umbrella and returned to the field to finish the game.

✓ They canceled the game and played it another day.

___ They acted like crocodiles and slid around the wet bases.

___ The coaches played the game while the players sat in the dugout.

71

Dog-Gone!

Directions: Read the story. Then, follow the instructions.

Scotty and Simone were washing their dog, Willis. His fur was wet. Their hands were wet. Willis did NOT like to be wet. Scotty dropped the soap. Simone picked it up and let go of Willis. Uh-oh!

1. Write what happened next.
   __Answers will vary__
2. Draw what happened next.

   Drawings will vary.

72

Game Time! 73

A **fact** is something that can be proven. An **opinion** is a feeling or belief about something and cannot be proven.

Directions: Read these sentences about different games. Then, write **F** next to each fact and **O** next to each opinion.

O 1. Tennis is cool!

F 2. There are red and black markers in a Checkers game.

F 3. In football, a touchdown is worth six points.

O 4. Being a goalie in soccer is easy.

F 5. A yo-yo moves on a string.

O 6. June's sister looks like the queen on the card.

F 7. The six kids need three more players for a baseball team.

O 8. Table tennis is more fun than court tennis.

Owls Are a Hoot 74

Directions: Read the story. Then, follow the instructions.

My name is Owen Owl, and I am a bird. I go to Nocturnal School. Our teacher is Mr. Screech Owl. In his class I learned that owls are birds and can sleep all day and hunt at night. Some of us live in nests in trees. In North America, it is against the law to harm owls. I like being an owl!

Write **F** next to each fact and **O** next to each opinion.

F 1. No one can harm owls in North America.

O 2. It would be great if owls could talk.

F 3. Owls sleep all day.

F 4. Some owls sleep in nests.

O 5. Mr. Screech Owl is a good teacher.

F 6. Owls are birds.

O 7. Owen Owl would be a good friend.

F 8. Owls hunt at night.

Chef Jeff 75

Directions: Read the story. Then, answer the questions.

Jeff is baking cookies. He wears special clothes when he bakes. He puts flour, sugar, eggs and butter into a bowl. He mixes everything together. He puts the cookies in the oven at 11:15 A.M. It takes 15 minutes for the cookies to bake. Jeff wants something cold and white to drink when he eats his cookies.

1. Is Jeff baking a cake?   Yes (No)

2. What are two things that Jeff might wear when he bakes?
(hat) boots (apron) tie raincoat roller skates

3. What didn't Jeff put in the cookies?
flour eggs (milk) butter sugar

4. What do you think Jeff does after he mixes the cookies but before he bakes them?
Answers may include: rolling dough into small balls or dropping dough from a teaspoon onto a cookie sheet.

5. What time will the cookies be done? 11:30 a.m.

6. What will Jeff drink with his cookies? milk

7. Why do you think Jeff wanted to bake cookies?
Answers will vary.

Mother's Helper 76

Directions: Read more about sea horses. Then, answer the questions.

A father sea horse helps the mother. He has a small sack or pouch, on the front of his body. The mother sea horse lays the eggs. She does not keep them. She gives the eggs to the father.

1. What does the mother sea horse do with her eggs?
She gives them to the father.

2. Where does the father sea horse put the eggs?
in his pouch

3. Sea horses can change color. Color the sea horses.

What Do You See? 77

Directions: Read this story about Ling and Bradley. Draw pictures for the beginning and middle to describe each part of the story.

Beginning: One sunny day, Ling and Bradley, wearing their empty backpacks, rode their bikes down the street to the park.

Drawings will vary.

Middle: They stopped by an oak tree with many acorns under it. They picked up some and stuffed them into their backpacks.

Drawings will vary.

Directions: Draw an ending for this story that tells what you think they did with the acorns.

End: With the heavy backpacks strapped on their backs, they pedaled home.

Drawings will vary.

It's No Problem! 78

Juniper has three problems to solve. She needs your help.

Directions: Read each problem. Write what you think she should do.

1. Juniper is watching her favorite TV show when the power goes out.
Answers will vary

2. Juniper is riding her bike to school when the front tire goes flat.
Answers will vary

3. Juniper loses her father while shopping in the supermarket.
Answers will vary

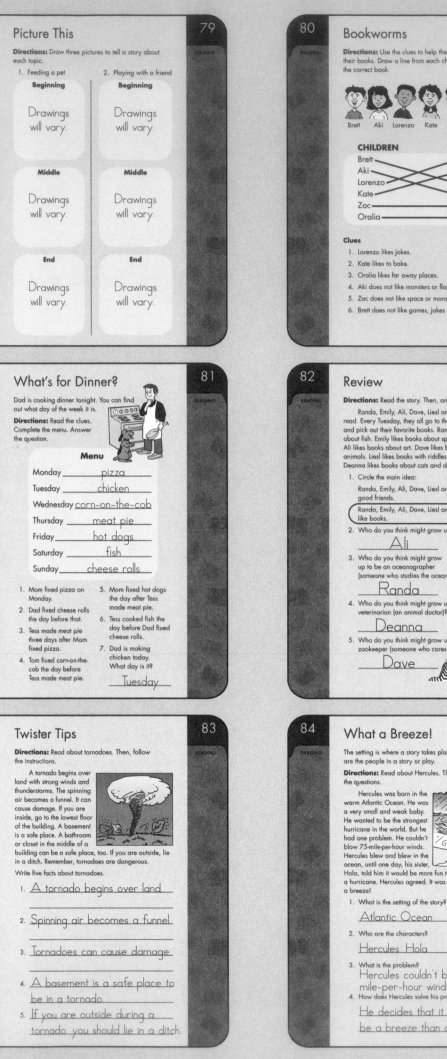

Picture This
79

Directions: Draw three pictures to tell a story about each topic.

1. Feeding a pet

Beginning

Drawings will vary.

Middle

Drawings will vary.

End

Drawings will vary.

2. Playing with a friend

Beginning

Drawings will vary.

Middle

Drawings will vary.

End

Drawings will vary.

Bookworms
80

Directions: Use the clues to help the children find their books. Draw a line from each child's name to the correct book.

Brett Aki Lorenzo Kate Zac Oralia

CHILDREN   **BOOKS**

Brett — jokes
Aki — cakes
Lorenzo — monsters
Kate — games
Zac — flags
Oralia — space

Clues

1. Lorenzo likes jokes.
2. Kate likes to bake.
3. Oralia likes far away places.
4. Aki does not like monsters or flags.
5. Zac does not like space or monsters.
6. Brett does not like games, jokes or cakes.

What's for Dinner?
81

Dad is cooking dinner tonight. You can find out what day of the week it is.

Directions: Read the clues. Complete the menu. Answer the question.

Menu

Monday _____ pizza
Tuesday _____ chicken
Wednesday _____ corn-on-the-cob
Thursday _____ meat pie
Friday _____ hot dogs
Saturday _____ fish
Sunday _____ cheese rolls

1. Mom fixed pizza on Monday.
2. Dad fixed cheese rolls the day before that.
3. Tess made meat pie three days after Mom fixed pizza.
4. Tom fixed corn-on-the-cob the day before Tess made meat pie.
5. Mom fixed hot dogs the day after Tess made meat pie.
6. Tess cooked fish the day before Dad fixed cheese rolls.
7. Dad is making chicken today. What day is it?

_____ Tuesday

Review
82

Directions: Read the story. Then, answer the questions.

Randa, Emily, Ali, Dave, Liesl and Deana all love to read. Every Tuesday, they all go to the library together and pick out their favorite books. Randa likes books about fish. Emily likes books about sports and athletes. Ali likes books about art. Dave likes books about wild animals. Liesl likes books with riddles and puzzles. Deanna likes books about cats and dogs.

1. Circle the main idea:

   Randa, Emily, Ali, Dave, Liesl and Deana are good friends.

   (Randa, Emily, Ali, Dave, Liesl and Deana all like books.)

2. Who do you think might grow up to be an artist?

   _____ Ali

3. Who do you think might grow up to be an oceanographer (someone who studies the ocean)?

   _____ Randa

4. Who do you think might grow up to be a veterinarian (an animal doctor)?

   _____ Deanna

5. Who do you think might grow up to be a zookeeper (someone who cares for zoo animals)?

   _____ Dave

Twister Tips
83

Directions: Read about tornadoes. Then, follow the instructions.

A tornado begins over land with strong winds and thunderstorms. The spinning air becomes a funnel. It can cause damage. If you are inside, go to the lowest floor of the building. A basement is a safe place. A bathroom or closet in the middle of a building can be a safe place, too. If you are outside, lie in a ditch. Remember, tornadoes are dangerous.

Write five facts about tornadoes.

1. A tornado begins over land.
2. Spinning air becomes a funnel.
3. Tornadoes can cause damage.
4. A basement is a safe place to be in a tornado.
5. If you are outside during a tornado, you should lie in a ditch.

What a Breeze!
84

The setting is where a story takes place. The characters are the people in a story or play.

Directions: Read about Hercules. Then, answer the questions.

Hercules was born in the warm Atlantic Ocean. He was a very small and weak baby. He wanted to be the strongest hurricane in the world. But he had one problem. He couldn't blow 75-mile-per-hour winds. Hercules blew and blew in the ocean, until one day, his sister, Hola, told him it would be more fun to be a breeze than a hurricane. Hercules agreed. It was a breeze to be a breeze!

1. What is the setting of the story?

   Atlantic Ocean

2. Who are the characters?

   Hercules, Hola

3. What is the problem?

   Hercules couldn't blow 75 mile-per-hour winds.

4. How does Hercules solve his problem?

   He decides that it is more fun to be a breeze than a hurricane

Red, White, and Blue — 85

Directions: Read each story. Then, write whether it is fiction or nonfiction.

One sunny day in July, a dog named Stan ran away from home. He went up one street and down the other looking for fun, but all the yards were empty. Where was everybody? Stan kept walking until he heard the sound of band music and happy people. Stan walked faster until he got to Central Street. There he saw men, women, children and dogs getting ready to walk in a parade. It was the Fourth of July!

Fiction or Nonfiction? **Fiction**

Americans celebrate the Fourth of July every year, because it is the birthday of the United States of America. On July 4, 1776, the United States got its independence from Great Britain. Today, Americans celebrate this holiday with parades, picnics and fireworks as they proudly wave the red, white and blue American flag.

Fiction or Nonfiction? **Nonfiction**

Hisssss! — 86

Directions: Write a fictional (make-believe) story about a snake. Make sure to include details and a title.

_____ title

Stories will vary.

Know Your ABCs — 88

Directions: Write these words in order. If two words start with the same letter, look at the second letter in each word.

Example: lamb Lamb comes first because **a** comes
light before **i** in the alphabet.

tree	branch
branch	leaf
leaf	tree

dish	bone
dog	dish
bone	dog

rain	cloud
umbrella	rain
cloud	umbrella

mail	mail
stamp	slot
slot	stamp

From A to Z — 89

If the first letters of two words are the same, look at the second letters in both words. If the second letters are the same, look at the third letters.

Directions: Write 1, 2, 3 or 4 on the lines in each row to put the words in ABC order.

Example:

1. **1** candy **2** carrot **4** duck **3** dance

2. **2** cold **4** hot **1** carry **3** hit

3. **2** flash **1** fan **3** fun **4** garden

4. **2** seat **4** sun **1** saw **3** sit

5. **3** row **1** ring **2** rock **4** run

6. **2** truck **3** turn **4** twin **1** talk

Friends and Family — 90

Directions: Write the following names in ABC order: Oscar, Ali, Lance, Kim, Zane and Bonita.

Ali
Bonita
Kim
Lance
Oscar
Zane

Directions: Write the names of six of your friends or family in ABC order.

Answers will vary

Super Similar — 91

Words that mean the same or nearly the same are called **synonyms**.

Directions: Read the sentence that tells about the picture. Draw a circle around the word that means the same as the **bold** word.

The child is **unhappy**.
(sad) hungry

The flowers are **lovely**.
(pretty) green

The baby was very **tired**.
(sleepy) hurt

The **funny** clown made us laugh.
(silly) glad

The ladybug is so **tiny**.
(small) red

We saw a **scary** tiger.
(frightening) ugly

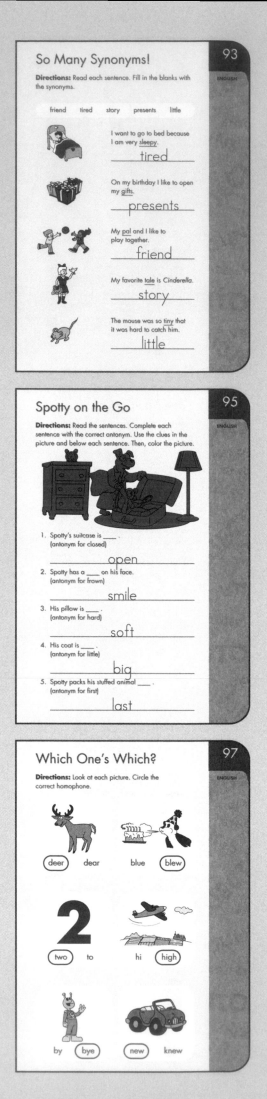

92 · A Silly Synonym Story

Synonyms are words that have almost the same meaning.

Directions: Read the story. Then, fill in the blanks with the synonyms.

> funny   unhappy
> windy   little

A New Balloon

It was a breezy day. The wind blew the small child's balloon away. The child was sad. A silly clown gave him a new balloon.

1. It was a ___windy___ day.
2. The wind blew the ___little___ child's balloon away.
3. The child was ___unhappy___.
4. A ___funny___ clown gave him a new balloon.

93 · So Many Synonyms!

Directions: Read each sentence. Fill in the blanks with the synonyms.

> friend   tired   story   presents   little

I want to go to bed because I am very <u>sleepy</u>.
___tired___

On my birthday I like to open my <u>gifts</u>.
___presents___

My <u>pal</u> and I like to play together.
___friend___

My favorite <u>tale</u> is *Cinderella*.
___story___

The mouse was so <u>tiny</u> that it was hard to catch him.
___little___

94 · All About Antonyms

Antonyms are words that mean the opposite of another word.

Examples:
hot and **cold**
short and **tall**

Directions: Draw a line from each word on the left to its antonym on the right.

sad — happy
bottom — top
black — white
tall — short
thin — fat
little — big
cold — hot
lost — found
go — stop
soft — hard

95 · Spotty on the Go

Directions: Read the sentences. Complete each sentence with the correct antonym. Use the clues in the picture and below each sentence. Then, color the picture.

1. Spotty's suitcase is ___. (antonym for closed)
   ___open___
2. Spotty has a ___ on his face. (antonym for frown)
   ___smile___
3. His pillow is ___. (antonym for hard)
   ___soft___
4. His coat is ___. (antonym for little)
   ___big___
5. Spotty packs his stuffed animal ___. (antonym for first)
   ___last___

96 · Hearing Homophones

Homophones are words that sound the same but are spelled differently and mean different things.

Directions: Write the homophone from the box next to each picture.

> so   see   blew   pear

sew ___so___

pair ___pear___

sea ___see___

blue ___blew___

97 · Which One's Which?

Directions: Look at each picture. Circle the correct homophone.

(deer)   dear   blue   (blew)

(two)   to   hi   (high)

by   (bye)   (new)   knew

98 Nouns I Know

A noun is the name of a person, place or thing.

Directions: Read the story and circle all the nouns. Then, write the nouns next to the pictures below.

Our family likes to go to the park.
family
park

We play on the swings.
swings

We eat cake.
cake

We drink lemonade.
lemonade

We throw the ball to our dog.
ball
dog

Then, we go home.
home

99 Nouns All Around

Directions: Look through a magazine. Cut out pictures of nouns and glue them below. Write the name of the noun next to the picture.

Nouns

Answers will vary.

100 Name-It Nouns

Proper nouns are the names of specific people, places and pets. Proper nouns begin with a capital letter.

Directions: Write the proper nouns on the lines below. Use capital letters at the beginning of each word.

logan, utah
Logan, Utah

mike smith
Mike Smith

lynn cramer
Lynn Cramer

buster
Buster

fluffy
Fluffy

chicago, illinois
Chicago, Illinois

101 It's a Date!

The days of the week and the months of the year are always capitalized.

Directions: Circle the words that are written correctly. Write the words that need capital letters on the lines below.

sunday (July) (Wednesday)
may december friday
tuesday june august
(Monday) january (February)
(March) (Thursday) (April)
(September) saturday (October)

Days of the Week
1. Sunday
2. Friday
3. Tuesday
4. Saturday

Months of the Year
1. January
2. June
3. May
4. August
5. December

102 A Capital Idea

The first word and all of the important words in a title begin with a capital letter.

Directions: Write the book titles on the lines below. Use capital letters.

1. Dinosaurs
2. Lizards Everywhere
3. The Magic Cat
4. All About Presidents
5. The Space Dog
6. Gerbil Care

103 A Number of Nouns

Plural nouns name more than one person, place or thing.

Directions: Read the words in the box. Write the words in the correct column.

hats girl cows kittens cake
poons glass book horse trees

girl hats
glass spoons
book cows
horse kittens
cake trees

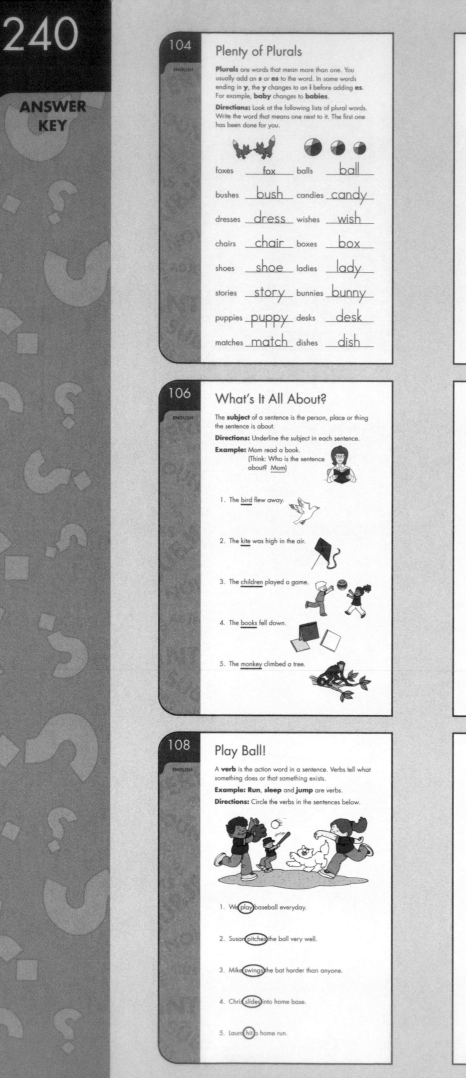

104 Plenty of Plurals

Plurals are words that mean more than one. You usually add an **s** or **es** to the word. In some words ending in **y**, the **y** changes to an **i** before adding **es**. For example, **baby** changes to **babies**.

Directions: Look at the following lists of plural words. Write the word that means one next to it. The first one has been done for you.

foxes	fox	balls	ball
bushes	bush	candies	candy
dresses	dress	wishes	wish
chairs	chair	boxes	box
shoes	shoe	ladies	lady
stories	story	bunnies	bunny
puppies	puppy	desks	desk
matches	match	dishes	dish

105 Pronoun Pros

Pronouns are words that can be used instead of nouns. **She**, **he**, **it** and **they** are pronouns.

Directions: Read the sentence. Then, write the sentence again, using **she**, **he**, **it** or **they** in the blank.

She   He   They   It

1. Dan likes funny jokes.

   He likes funny jokes.

2. Peg and Sam went to the zoo.

   They went to the zoo.

3. My dog likes to dig in the yard.

   It likes to dig in the yard.

4. Sara is a very good dancer.

   She is a very good dancer.

5. Fred and Ted are twins.

   They are twins.

106 What's It All About?

The **subject** of a sentence is the person, place or thing the sentence is about.

Directions: Underline the subject in each sentence.

Example: Mom read a book.
(Think: Who is the sentence about? Mom)

1. The bird flew away.

2. The kite was high in the air.

3. The children played a game.

4. The books fell down.

5. The monkey climbed a tree.

107 Double Up

Two similar sentences can be joined into one sentence if the predicate is the same. A **compound subject** is made up of two subjects joined together by the word **and**.

Example: Jamie can sing.
Sandy can sing.
Jamie **and** Sandy can sing.

Directions: Combine the sentences. Write the new sentence on the line.

1. The cats are my pets.
   The dogs are my pets.

   The cats and dogs are my pets.

2. Chairs are in the store.
   Tables are in the store.

   Chairs and tables are in the store.

3. Tom can ride a bike.
   Jack can ride a bike.

   Tom and Jack can ride a bike.

108 Play Ball!

A **verb** is the action word in a sentence. Verbs tell what something does or that something exists.

Example: **Run**, **sleep** and **jump** are verbs.

Directions: Circle the verbs in the sentences below.

1. We play baseball everyday.

2. Susan pitches the ball very well.

3. Mike swings the bat harder than anyone.

4. Chris slides into home base.

5. Laura hit a home run.

109 Verb Alert!

We use verbs to tell when something happens. Sometimes we add an **ed** to verbs that tell us if something has already happened.

Example: Today, we will **play**. Yesterday, we **played**.

Directions: Write the correct verb in the blank.

1. Today, I will wash my dog, Fritz.
   wash   washed

2. Last week, Fritz cried when we said, "Bath time, Fritz."
   cry   cried

3. My sister likes to help wash Fritz.
   help   helped

4. One time she cleaned Fritz by herself.
   clean   cleaned

5. Fritz will look a lot better after his bath.
   look   looked

110 Predicate Power

The **predicate** is the part of the sentence that tells about the action.

Directions: Circle the predicate in each sentence.

Example: The boys ran on the playground.
(Think: The boys did what? Ran)

1. The woman (painted) a picture.

2. The puppy (chases) his ball.

3. The students (went) to school.

4. Butterflies (fly) in the air.

5. The baby (wants) a drink.

111 Twice the Action

A **compound predicate** is made by joining two sentences that have the same subject. The predicates are joined together by the word **and**.

Example: Tom can jump.
Tom can run.
Tom can run **and** jump.

Directions: Combine the sentences. Write the new sentence on the line.

1. The dog can roll over.
The dog can bark.
The dog can roll over and bark.

2. My mom plays with me.
My mom reads with me.
My mom plays and reads with me.

3. Tara is tall.
Tara is smart.
Tara is tall and smart.

112 School Days

The **subject** part of the sentence is the person, place or thing the sentence is about. The **predicate** is the part of the sentence that tells what the subject does.

Directions: Draw a line between the subject and the predicate. Underline the noun in the subject and circle the verb.

Example: The furry <u>cat</u> | (ate) food.

1. <u>Mandi</u> | (walks) to school.

2. The <u>bus</u> | (drove) the children.

3. The school <u>bell</u> | (rang) very loudly.

4. The <u>teacher</u> | (spoke) to the students.

5. The <u>girls</u> | (opened) their books.

113 All Together Now

Directions: Write one new sentence using a compound subject or predicate.

Example: The boy will jump. The girl will jump.
The <u>boy and girl</u> will jump.

1. The clowns run. The clowns play.
The clowns run and play.

2. The dogs dance. The bears dance.
The dogs and bears dance.

3. Seals bark. Seals clap.
Seals bark and clap.

4. The girls play. The girls laugh.
The girls play and laugh.

114 Ready to Roll

Directions: Draw a circle around the noun, the naming part of the sentence. Draw a line under the verb, the action part of the sentence.

Example: (John) <u>drinks</u> juice every morning.

1. Our (class) <u>skates</u> at the roller-skating rink.

2. (Miguel) and (Emma) <u>go</u> very fast.

3. (Austin) <u>eats</u> hot dogs.

4. (Sierra) <u>dances</u> to the music.

5. (Everyone) <u>likes</u> the skating rink.

115 Tell Me More!

Adjectives are words that tell more about a person, place or thing.

Examples: cold, fuzzy, dark

Directions: Circle the adjectives in the sentences.

1. The (juicy) apple is on the plate.

2. The (furry) dog is eating a bone.

3. It was a (sunny) day.

4. The kitten drinks (warm) milk.

5. The baby has a (loud) cry.

116 — A Day on the Farm

Directions: Choose an adjective from the box to fill in the blanks.

hungry	sunny	busy	funny
fresh	deep	pretty	cloudy

1. It is a **sunny** day on Farmer Brown's farm.

2. Farmer Brown is a very **busy** man.

3. Mrs. Brown likes to feed the **hungry** chickens.

4. Every day she collects the **fresh** eggs.

5. The ducks swim in the **deep** pond.

117 — Make a Wish!

Articles are small words that help us to better understand nouns. **A** and **an** are articles. We use **an** before a word that begins with a vowel. We use a before a word that begins with a consonant.

Example: We looked in **a** nest. It had **an** eagle in it.

Directions: Read the sentences. Write a or an in the blank.

1. I found **a** book.

2. It had a story about **an** ant in it.

3. In the story, **a** lion gave three wishes to ant.

4. The ant's first wish was to ride **an** elephant.

5. The second wish was to ride **an** alligator.

6. The last wish was **a** wish for three more wishes.

118 — Sentence Sense

A **sentence** tells a complete idea. It has a noun and a verb. It begins with a capital letter and has punctuation at the end.

Directions: Circle the group of words if it is a sentence.

1. (Grass is a green plant.)

2. Mowing the lawn.

3. (Grass grows in fields and lawns.)

4. Tickle the feet.

5. (Sheep, cows and horses eat grass.)

6. We like to play in.

7. (My sister likes to mow the lawn.)

8. A picnic on the grass.

119 — Making a Statement

Statements are sentences that tell us something. They begin with a capital letter and end with a period.

Directions: Write the sentences on the lines below. Begin each sentence with a capital letter and end it with a period.

1. we like to ride our bikes
   We like to ride our bikes.

2. we go down the hill very fast
   We go down the hill very fast.

3. we keep our bikes shiny and clean
   We keep our bikes shiny and clean.

4. we know how to change the tires
   We know how to change the tires.

120 — Ask Me a Question

Questions are sentences that ask something. They begin with a capital letter and end with a question mark.

Directions: Write the questions on the lines below. Begin each sentence with a capital letter and end it with a question mark.

1. will you be my friend
   Will you be my friend?

2. what is your name
   What is your name?

3. are you eight years old
   Are you eight years old?

4. do you like rainbows
   Do you like rainbows?

121 — What a Surprise!

Surprising sentences tell a strong feeling and end with an exclamation point. A surprising sentence may be only one or two words showing fear, surprise or pain.
Example: Oh, no!

Directions: Put a period at the end of the sentences that tell something. Put an exclamation point at the end of the sentences that tell a strong feeling. Put a question mark at the end of the sentences that ask a question.

1. The cheetah can run very fast.

2. Wow!

3. Look at that cheetah go!

4. Can you run fast?

5. Oh, my!

6. You're faster than I am.

7. Let's run together.

8. We can run as fast as a cheetah.

9. What fun!

10. Do you think cheetahs get tired?

122 That's Mine!

We add **'s** to nouns (people, places or things) to tell who or what owns something.

Directions: Read the sentences. Fill in the blanks to show ownership.

Example: The doll belongs to **Sara**.

It is **Sara's** doll.

1. Sparky has a red collar.

   Sparky's collar is red.

2. Jimmy has a blue coat.

   Jimmy's coat is blue.

3. The tail of the cat is short.

   The _cat's_ tail is short.

4. The name of my mother is Karen.

   My _mother's_ name is Karen.

123 Owning Up

Directions: Read the sentences. Choose the correct word and write it in the sentences below.

1. The _boy's_ lunchbox is broken.
   boys / boy's

2. The _gerbils_ played in the cage.
   gerbil's   gerbils

3. _Ann's_ hair is brown.
   Anns   Ann's

4. The _horses_ ran in the field.
   horse's   horses

5. My _sister's_ coat is torn.
   sister's   sisters

6. The _cat's_ fur is brown.
   cats   cat's

7. Three _birds_ flew past our window.
   birds   bird's

8. The _dog's_ paws are muddy.
   dogs   dog's

124 Look It Up

A dictionary is a book that gives the meaning of words. It also tells how words sound. Words in a dictionary are in ABC order. That makes them easier to find. A picture dictionary lists a word, a picture of the word and its meaning.

Directions: Look at this page from a picture dictionary. Then, answer the questions.

baby	**band**	**bank**
A very young child.	A group of people who play music.	A place where money is kept.
bark	**berry**	**board**
The sound a dog makes.	A small, juicy fruit.	A flat piece of wood.

1. What is a small, juicy fruit? _berry_

2. What is a group of people who play music? _band_

3. What is the name for a very young child? _baby_

4. What is a flat piece of wood called? _board_

125 Word to Word

The guide words at the top of a page in a dictionary tell you what the first and last words on the page will be. Only words that come in ABC order between those two words will be on that page. Guide words help you find the page you need to look up a word.

Directions: Write each word from the box in ABC order between each pair of guide words.

faint	far	fence	feed	farmer
fan	feet	farm	family	face

face   **fence**

few	_first_
fierce	_fish_
fight	_fix_
fill	_flat_
finish	_flush_

126 Many Meanings

When words have more than one meaning, the meanings are numbered in a dictionary.

Directions: Read the meanings of **tag**. Write the number of the correct definition after each sentence.

tag

1. A small strip or tab attached to something else.

2. To label.

3. To follow closely and constantly.

4. A game of chase.

1. We will play a game of tag after we study. _4_

2. I will tag this coat with its price. _2_

3. My little brother will tag along with us. _3_

4. My mother already took off the price tag. _1_

5. The tag on the puppy said, "For Sale." _1_

6. Do not tag that tree. _2_

128 Number Names

Directions: Write each number word beside the correct picture. Then, write it again.

Example:

six   six

one   two   three   four   five   six   seven   eight   nine   ten

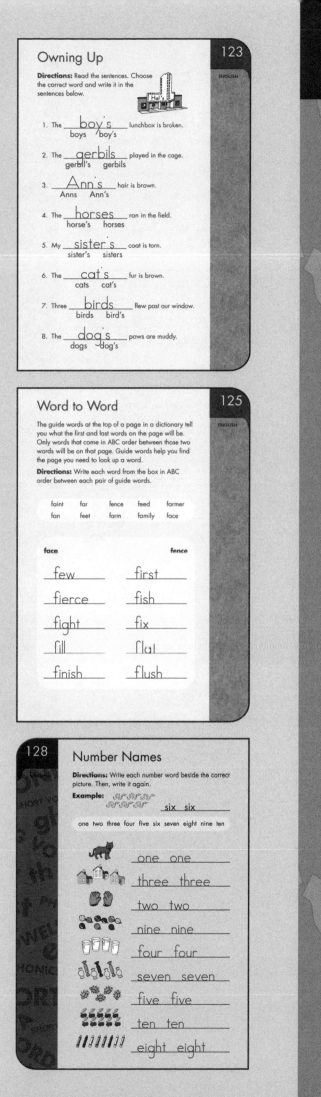

one   one

three   three

two   two

nine   nine

four   four

seven   seven

five   five

ten   ten

eight   eight

Say It With Numbers 129

Directions: Change the telling sentences into asking sentences. Change the asking sentences into telling sentences. Begin each one with a capital letter and end it with a period or a question mark.

Examples:

Is she eating three cookies?

__She is eating three cookies.__

He is bringing one truck.

__Is he bringing one truck?__

1. Is he painting two bluebirds?

   __He is painting two bluebirds.__

2. Did she find four apples?

   __She did find four apples.__

3. She will be six on her birthday.

   __Is she six on her birthday?__ *(handwritten: She will be six on her birthday.)*

Super Sounds: Short a 130

Directions: Use a word from the box to complete each sentence.

fat	path	lamp	can
van	stamp	Dan	math
sat	cat	fan	bat

Example:

1. The __lamp__ had a pink shade.
2. The bike __path__ led us to the park.
3. I like to add in __math__ class.
4. The cat is very __fat__.
5. The __can__ of beans was hard to open.
6. The envelope needed a __stamp__.
7. He swung the __bat__ and hit the ball.
8. The __fan__ blew air around.
9. My mom drives a blue __van__.
10. I __sat__ in the backseat.

Super Sounds: Long a 131

Long a is the vowel sound which says its own name. **Long a** can be spelled **ai** as in the word **mail**, **ay** as in the word **say** and **a** with a **silent e** at the end of a word as in the word **same**.

Directions: Say each word and listen for the **long a** sound. Then, write each word and underline the letters that make the **long a** vowel sound.

mail	bake	train
game	day	sale
paint	play	name
made	gray	tray

1. __mail__
2. __paint__
3. __game__
4. __made__
5. __bake__
6. __play__
7. __day__
8. __gray__
9. __train__
10. __name__
11. __sale__
12. __tray__

Super Sounds: Short e 132

Directions: Write the correct short e word in each sentence.

get	Meg	rest	bed	spent
test	head	pet	red	best

1. Of all my crayons, I like the __red__ color the __best__.
2. I always make my __bed__ when I __get__ up.
3. My new hat keeps my __head__ warm.
4. __Meg__ wanted a dog for a __pet__.
5. I have a __test__ in math tomorrow, so I want to get a good night's __sleep__.

Super Sounds: Long e 133

Long e is the vowel sound which says its own name. **Long e** can be spelled **ee** as in the word **teeth**, **ea** as in the word **meat** or **e** as in the word **me**.

Directions: Say each word and listen for the **long e** sound. Then, write the words and underline the letters that make the **long e** sound.

street	neat	treat
feet	sleep	keep
deal	meal	mean
clean	beast	feast

1. __street__
2. __sleep__
3. __mean__
4. __neat__
5. __keep__
6. __clean__
7. __treat__
8. __deal__
9. __beast__
10. __feet__
11. __meal__
12. __feast__

Super Sounds: Short i 134

Short i is the sound you hear in the word **pin**.

Directions: Use the **short i** words in the box to write rhyming words.

pin	fin	win	fish
pitch	wish	rich	kick
ship	dip	dish	sick

1. Write the words that rhyme with **spin**.

   __pin__ __fin__ __win__

2. Write the words that rhyme with **ditch**.

   __pitch__ __rich__

3. Write the words that rhyme with **rip**.

   __ship__ __dip__

4. Write the words that rhyme with **squish**.

   __wish__ __dish__ __fish__

5. Write the words that rhyme with **lick**.

   __kick__ __sick__

135 — Super Sounds: Long i

Long i is the vowel sound which says its own name. **Long i** can be spelled **igh** as in **sight**, **i** with a **silent e** at the end as in **mine** and **y** at the end as in **fly**.

Directions: Say each word and listen for the **long i** sound. Then, write each word and underline the letters that make the **long i** sound.

bike	hike	ride
line	glide	ripe
nine	pipe	fight
high	light	sigh

1. <u>bike</u>   7. <u>ride</u>
2. <u>glide</u>   8. <u>nine</u>
3. <u>fight</u>   9. <u>light</u>
4. <u>hike</u>   10. <u>line</u>
5. <u>ripe</u>   11. <u>pipe</u>
6. <u>high</u>   12. <u>sigh</u>

136 — Super Sounds: Short o

Short o is the vowel sound you hear in the word **got**.
Directions: Use the **short o** words in the box to write rhyming words.

hot	rock
lock	cot
stop	sock
fox	mop
box	clock

1. Write the words that rhyme with **dot**.
   <u>hot</u>   <u>cot</u>

2. Write the words that rhyme with **socks**.
   <u>box</u>   <u>fox</u>

3. Write the words that rhyme with **hop**.
   <u>stop</u>   <u>mop</u>

4. Write the words that rhyme with **dock**.
   <u>rock</u>   <u>sock</u>
   <u>lock</u>   <u>clock</u>

137 — Super Sounds: Long o

Directions: Draw a line from the first part of the sentence to the part which completes the sentence.

1. Do you know — in the water.
2. The dog — was in the tree.
3. The boat floats — who wrote the note?
4. I hope the phone — has a bone.
5. Carol's ice-cream cone — rings soon for me!
6. The rope swing — a coat in the cold.
7. I had to wear — was melting.

138 — Super Sounds: Short u

Directions: Circle the words in each sentence which are not correct. Then, write the correct **short u** words from the box on the lines.

tub	cub	bump
pump	bug	dust
cut	must	nut
jump	rug	hug

1. The (crust) made me sneeze.
   <u>dust</u>

2. I need to take a bath in the (cub).
   <u>tub</u>

3. The (mug) bite left a big (pump) on my arm.
   <u>bug</u>   <u>bump</u>

4. It is time to get my hair (hut).
   <u>cut</u>

5. The mother bear took care of her (shrub).
   <u>cub</u>

6. We need to (jump) more gas into the car.
   <u>pump</u>

139 — Super Sounds: Long u

Long u is the vowel sound you hear in the word **cube**. Another vowel sound which is very much like the **long u** sound is the **oo** sound you hear in the word **boot**.

Directions: Use the **long u** and **oo** words in the box to write rhyming words.

moon	use	blew
flew	loose	choose
fuse	noon	goose

1. Write the words that rhyme with **soon**.
   <u>moon</u>   <u>noon</u>

2. Write the words that rhyme with **lose**.
   <u>fuse</u>   <u>use</u>   <u>choose</u>

3. Write the words that rhyme with **grew**.
   <u>flew</u>   <u>blew</u>

4. Write the words that rhyme with **moose**.
   <u>loose</u>   <u>goose</u>

140 — Ready, Set, Action!

Verbs are words that tell the action in the sentence.
Directions: Draw a line from each sentence to its picture. Then, finish the sentence with the verb or action word that is under each picture.

Example:
He will <u>help</u> the baby.

carry

1. I can <u>fix</u> my book.
   help

2. It is time to <u>clean</u> up.
   cut

3. That chair might <u>break</u>.
   build

4. They <u>build</u> houses.
   clean

5. I <u>cut</u> this out myself.
   fix

6. Is that too heavy to <u>carry</u>?
   break

How Does It End? | 141

Most **verbs** end with **s** when the sentence tells about one thing. The **s** is taken away when the sentence tells about more than one thing.

Example:

One dog walks.   One boy runs.
Two dogs **walk**.   Three boys **run**.

The spelling of some **verbs** changes when the sentence tells about only one thing.

One girl carries her lunch.   The boy fixes his car.
Two girls **carry** their lunches.   The boys **fix** their cars.

Directions: Write the missing verbs in the sentences.

Example:

Pam works hard. She and Peter ___work___ all day.

1. The father bird builds a nest.

   The mother and father ___build___ it together.

2. The girls clean their room.

   Jenny ___cleans___ under her bed.

3. The children cut out their pictures.

   Henry ___cuts___ his slowly.

4. These workers fix things.

   This man ___fixes___ televisions.

5. Two trucks carry horses.

   One truck ___carries___ pigs.

---

142 | Animal Action

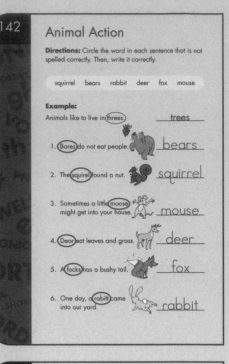

Directions: Circle the word in each sentence that is not spelled correctly. Then, write it correctly.

squirrel   bears   rabbit   deer   fox   mouse

Example:

Animals like to live in (threes).   ___trees___

1. (Bares) do not eat people.   ___bears___

2. The (squirrel) found a nut.   ___squirrel___

3. Sometimes a little (moose) might get into your house.   ___mouse___

4. (Dear) eat leaves and grass.   ___deer___

5. A (focks) has a bushy tail.   ___fox___

6. One day, a (rabbit) came into our yard.   ___rabbit___

Lots of Animals | 143

Directions: Write the two sentences below as one sentence. Remember the special spelling of **fox**, **mouse** and **deer** when there are more than one.

Example:

I saw a mouse. You saw a mouse.

___We saw two mice.___

1. Julie petted a deer.
   Matt petted a deer.

   ___Julie and Matt petted a deer.___

2. Mike colored a fox.
   Kim colored a fox.

   ___Mike and Kim colored two foxes.___

---

144 | All in the Family

Directions: This is Andy's **family tree**. It shows all the people in his family. Use the words in the box to finish writing the names in Andy's family tree.

grandmother   mother
grandfather   father
aunt   uncle
brother   sister

grandmother   grandfather   ___grandmother___   ___grandfather___

aunt   ___uncle___   my mother   my father   ___aunt___   uncle

sister   brother   me – Andy   ___sister___   ___brother___

Once Upon a Family | 145

Directions: Write the family words in the blanks to complete the story.

One day, my family had a picnic. My

___grandmother___ baked chicken.

___grandfather___ baked some rolls.

My ___uncle___ Jack brought corn. My

___aunt___ made something green and white in a big dish. I ate the chicken my

___grandmother___ brought. I had two rolls made

by my ___grandfather___. My ___uncle___ gave me some corn. I liked it all! Then, my

___brother___ and I looked in the dish my

___aunt___ had brought. "Did you try it?" I asked him.

"You're my big ___sister___," he said. "You try it!" I put a tiny bit in my mouth. It tasted good! But the dish was almost empty.

"It's terrible!" I said. "I'll eat the rest of it so you

won't have to. That's what a big ___sister___

is for!" My ___brother___ watched me eat it all. I tried not to look too happy!

---

146 | Where in the World?

Directions: Draw a line from each sentence to its picture. Then, complete each sentence with the word under the picture.

Example:

He is walking ___behind___ the tree.

outside

1. We stay ___inside___ when it rains.

behind

2. She drew a dog ___beside___ his house.

between

3. She stands ___between___ her friends.

across

4. They walked ___across___ the bridge.

around

5. Let the cat go ___outside___.

beside

6. Draw a circle ___around___ the fish.

inside

Find That Cat! 147

Directions: Use a location word to tell where the cat is in each sentence.

Example:

The cat is behind the box.

The cat is inside the cage.

The cat is between the dogs.

The cat is beside the mouse.

The cat is outside in the rain.

Heads or Tails? 148

Directions: Opposites are words which are different in every way. Use the opposite word from the box to complete these sentences.

hard   hot   bottom   quickly   happy
sad   slowly   cold   soft   top

Example:

My new coat is blue on __top__ and red on the __bottom__.

1. Snow is __cold__, but fire is __hot__.

2. A rabbit runs __quickly__, but a turtle moves __slowly__.

3. A bed is __soft__, but a floor is __hard__.

4. I feel __happy__ when my friends come and __sad__ when they leave.

A Sweet Surprise 149

Directions: Write opposite words in the blanks to complete the story.

hot   hard   top   cold   slowly
soft   quickly   happy   bottom   sad

One day, Grandma came for a visit. She gave my sister Jenny and me a box of chocolate candy. We said, "Thank you!" Then, Jenny __quickly__ took the __top__ off the box. The pieces all looked the same! I couldn't tell which pieces were __soft__ inside and which were __hard__! I only liked the __soft__ ones. Jenny didn't care. She was __happy__ to get any kind of candy!

I __slowly__ looked at all the pieces. I didn't know which one to pick. Just then Dad called us. Grandma was going home. He wanted us to say good-bye to her. I hurried to the front door where they were standing. Jenny came a minute later.

I told Grandma I hoped I would see her soon. I always feel __sad__ when she leaves. Jenny stood behind me and didn't say anything. After Grandma went home, I found out why. Jenny had most of our candy in her mouth! Only a few pieces were left in the __bottom__ of the box! Then, I was __sad__! That Jenny!

Tick, Tock, Time 150

The time between breakfast and lunch is **morning**.
The time between lunch and dinner is **afternoon**.
The time between dinner and bedtime is **evening**.

Directions: Write a time word from the box to complete each sentence. Use each word only once.

evening   morning   today   tomorrow   afternoon

1. What did you eat for breakfast this __morning__?

2. We came home from school in the __afternoon__.

3. I help wash the dinner dishes in the __evening__.

4. I feel a little tired __today__.

5. If I rest tonight, I will feel better __tomorrow__.

What Time Is It? 151

Directions: Write a sentence for these time words. Tell something you do at that time.

Example:

day

Every day I walk to school.

Answers will vary, but may include:

morning

I wake up early in the morning.

afternoon

I play outside in the afternoon.

evening

In the evening I watch T.V.

Review 152

Directions: Write the story below again and correct all the mistakes. Watch for words that are not spelled correctly, missing periods and question marks, question marks at the end of telling sentences and sentences with the wrong joining words.

One mourning, my granmother said I could have a pet mouse. That evening, we got my mouse at the pet store, or the next afernoon my mouse had babies! Now, I had nyne mouses! I really liked to wach them? I wanted to pick the babies up, and they were too little. When they get bigger, I have to give too mouses to my sisster.

One morning, my grandmother said I could have a pet mouse. That evening, we got my mouse at the pet store, and the next afternoon my mouse had babies! Now, I had nine mice! I really liked to watch them. I wanted to pick the babies up, but they were too little. When they get bigger, I have to give two mice to my sister.

248

ANSWER KEY

---

154 — Shape Escape!

MATH

Directions: Complete each row by drawing the correct shape.

155 — Pick a Pattern

MATH

Mia likes to count by twos, threes, fours, fives, tens and hundreds.

Directions: Complete the number patterns.

1. 5, _10_, _15_, 20, _25_, _30_, 35, _40_, _45_, 50
2. 100, _200_, _300_, 400, _500_, _600_, _700_, 800, _900_
3. _2_, 4, 6, _8_, _10_, 12, _14_, 16, _18_, _20_
4. 10, _20_, _30_, 40, _50_, _60_, 70, _80_, 90
5. 4, _8_, 12, _16_, _20_, 24, _28_, 32, _36_, 40

Directions: Make up two of your own number patterns.
Answers will vary.

156 — All Aboard!

MATH

Ordinal numbers indicate order in a series, such as **first**, **second** or **third**.

Directions: Follow the instructions to color the train cars. The first car is the engine.

Color the third car **blue**.
Color the eighth car **green**.
Color the fifth car **orange**.
Color the sixth car **yellow**.
Color the fourth car **brown**.
Color the second car **purple**.
Color the first car **red**.
Color the seventh car **pink**.

157 — Add Attack!

MATH

Addition is "putting together" or adding two or more numbers to find the sum.

Directions: Add.

Example:
2
+5
7

3	6	7	8	5
+4	+2	+1	+2	+4
7	8	8	10	9

8	9	10	6	4
+2	+5	+3	+6	+9
10	14	13	12	13

9	8	6	7	7
+3	+7	+5	+9	+6
12	15	11	16	13

158 — Add Attack: Forward and Back

MATH

The commutative property of addition states that even if the order of the numbers is changed in an addition sentence, the sum will stay tye same.

Example: 2 + 3 = 5
3 + 2 = 5

Directions: Look at the addition sentences below. Complete the addition sentences by writing the missing numerals.

5 + 4 = 9   3 + 1 = 4
4 + _5_ = 9   1 + _3_ = 4
2 + 6 = 8   6 + 1 = 7
6 + _2_ = 8   1 + _6_ = 7

Now try these:

6 + 3 = 9   10 + 2 = 12
_3_ + _6_ = 9   _2_ + _10_ = 12

Look at these sums. Can you think of two number sentences that would show the commutative property of addition. Answers will vary.

___ + ___ = 7   ___ + ___ = 11
___ + ___ = 7   ___ + ___ = 11

159 — Add Attack: 3 or More Numbers

MATH

Directions: Add all the numbers to find the sum. Draw pictures to help or break up the problem into two smaller problems.

Example:
1 ○
2 ○○
+3 ○○○
6

2 ⟩ 7
+5
2 ⟩ +6
+4 ⟩ 13

3 ⟩ 9
6
+2
11

8
2 ⟩ 9
+4
17

3 ⟩ 4
1
+5
9

8 ⟩ 10
2
+9
19

2 ⟩ 10
8
4 ⟩ +7
+3
17

3 ⟩ 9
6
5 ⟩ +7
+2
16

4 ⟩ 5
1
2 ⟩ +7
+5
12

6 ⟩ 13
7
3 ⟩ +4
+1
17

249

ANSWER
KEY

160 Take It Away!

MATH

Subtraction is "taking away" or subtracting one number from another to find the difference.

Directions: Subtract.

Example:

$$\begin{array}{r} 4 \\ -3 \\ \hline 1 \end{array}$$

5	6	4	3	2
-3	-1	-3	-1	-0
2	**5**	**1**	**2**	**2**

9	7	10	14	15
-2	-4	-5	-6	-9
7	**3**	**5**	**8**	**6**

18	13	14	11	17
-8	-5	-7	-4	-9
10	**8**	**7**	**7**	**8**

161 Find Your Place

MATH

The place value of a digit or numeral is shown by where it is in the number. For example, in the number **23**, **2** has the place value of **tens**, and **3** is **ones**.

Directions: Add the tens and ones and write your answers in the blanks.

Example:

3 tens + 3 ones = **33** = **33**

tens ones

7 tens + 5 ones = **75**   4 tens + 0 ones = **40**

2 tens + 3 ones = **23**   8 tens + 1 one = **81**

5 tens + 2 ones = **52**   1 ten + 1 one = **11**

5 tens + 4 ones = **54**   6 tens + 3 ones = **63**

Directions: Draw a line to the correct number.

6 tens + 7 ones — 73
4 tens + 2 ones — 67
8 tens + 0 ones — 51
7 tens + 3 ones — 80
5 tens + 1 one — 42

162 Add Attack: 2 Digits

MATH

Directions: Study the example. Follow the steps to add.

Example:

$$\begin{array}{r} 33 \\ +41 \\ \hline \end{array}$$

Step 1: Add the ones.   **Step 2:** Add the tens.

tens	ones
3	3
+4	1
	4

tens	ones
3	3
+4	1
7	4

tens	ones
4	2
+2	4
6	6

tens	ones
5	0
+4	7
9	7

24	15	38	11	37
+62	+23	+61	+26	+42
86	**38**	**99**	**37**	**79**

25	62	32	25	82
+42	+14	+44	+13	+6
67	**76**	**76**	**38**	**88**

163 Add Attack: 2 Digits

MATH

Directions: Add the total points scored in each game. Remember to add **ones** first and **tens** second.

Example:

HOME 22
VISITOR 17   Total **39**

HOME 28 / VISITOR 30   Total **58**
HOME 55 / VISITOR 21   Total **76**
HOME 14 / VISITOR 33   Total **47**

HOME 24 / VISITOR 13   Total **37**
HOME 46 / VISITOR 32   Total **78**
HOME 83 / VISITOR 06   Total **89**

HOME 30 / VISITOR 20   Total **50**
HOME 17 / VISITOR 42   Total **59**
HOME 24 / VISITOR 45   Total **69**

164 Add Attack: 2 Digits

MATH

Addition is "putting together" or adding two or more numbers to find the sum. Regrouping is using **ten ones** to form **one ten**, **ten tens** to form **one 100**, **fifteen ones** to form **one ten** and **five ones** and so on.

Directions: Study the examples. Follow the steps to add.

Example:

$$\begin{array}{r} 14 \\ +8 \\ \hline \end{array}$$

Step 1: Add the ones.   **Step 2:** Regroup the tens.   **Step 3:** Add the tens.

tens	ones
1	4
+	8
	12

tens	ones
1	
1	4
+	8
	2

tens	ones
1	
1	4
+	8
2	2

tens	ones
1	
1	6
+3	7
5	3

tens	ones
3	8
+5	3
9	1

tens	ones
1	
2	4
+4	7
7	1

28	32	54	19	44
+17	+38	+25	+55	+48
45	**70**	**79**	**74**	**92**

165 Add Attack: 2 Digits

MATH

Directions: Add the total points scored in the game. Remember to add the ones, regroup, and then add the tens.

Example:

HOME 47
VISITOR 38   Total **85**

HOME 33 / VISITOR 57   Total **90**
HOME 43 / VISITOR 49   Total **92**
HOME 57 / VISITOR 34   Total **91**

HOME 29 / VISITOR 22   Total **51**
HOME 36 / VISITOR 58   Total **94**
HOME 45 / VISITOR 39   Total **84**

HOME 66 / VISITOR 26   Total **92**
HOME 72 / VISITOR 19   Total **91**
HOME 54 / VISITOR 26   Total **80**

166 — Take It Away: 2 Digits

Directions: Study the example. Follow the steps to subtract.

Example:

```
  28
 -14
```

Step 1: Subtract the ones. **Step 2:** Subtract the tens.

tens	ones
2	8
-1	4
	4

tens	ones
2	8
-1	4
1	4

tens	ones
2	4
-1	2
1	2

tens	ones
3	8
-1	5
2	3

```
 24     61     77     85     57
-12    -30    -44    -24    -23
 12     31     33     61     34
```

```
 29     74     46     69     95
-15    -51    -32    -35    -32
 14     23     14     34     63
```

167 — Take It Away: 2 Digits

Directions: Study the steps for subtracting. Solve the problems using the steps.

Steps for Subtracting

1. Do you regroup? Yes, when the bottom number is bigger than the top.

tens	ones
3 X	12
-2	4
1	8

Regroup? Yes

tens	ones
3	7
-1	4
2	3

Regroup? No

2. Subtract the ones.
3. Subtract the tens.

```
 47      64      53
-28     -34     -39
 19      30      14
```

```
 56     83     43     75     91
-27    -47    -39    -53    -18
 29     36      4     22     73
```

```
 73     35     67     26     68
-66    -14    -58     -7    -45
  7     21      9     19     23
```

168 — Review

Directions: Add or subtract. Use regrouping when needed. Always do ones first and tens last.

```
tens ones   tens ones   tens ones
 9  3        3  0        6  5
-2  5       +2  7       +1  7
 6  8        5  7        8  2
```

```
 7  6        8  2        5  6
-2  8       +1  9       -2  8
 4  8       10  1        2  8
```

```
 4  3        5  3        2  4
-1  4       -1  5       +5  7
 2  9        3  8        8  1
```

```
 33          52          46
+47         +29         -37
 80          81           9
```

169 — Hundreds of Places

The place value of a digit or numeral is shown by where it is in the number. For example, in the number **123**, **1** has the place value of **hundreds**, **2** is **tens** and **3** is **ones**.

Directions: Study the examples. Then, write the missing numbers in the blanks.

Examples:

2 hundreds + 3 tens + 6 ones =

hundreds	tens	ones
2	3	6

= **236**

1 hundreds + 4 tens + 9 ones =

hundreds	tens	ones
1	4	9

= **149**

	hundreds	tens	ones	total
3 hundreds + 4 tens + 8 ones =	3	4	8	**348**
2 hundreds + 1 tens + **7** ones =	2	1	7	**217**
6 hundreds + **3** tens + 5 ones =	6	3	5	**635**
4 hundreds + **7** tens + 9 ones =	4	7	9	**479**
2 hundreds + **9** tens + **4** ones =	2	9	4	**294**
4 hundreds + 5 tens + 6 ones =	4	**5**	**6**	**456**
3 hundreds + 1 ten + 3 ones =	**3**	**1**	**3**	**313**
3 hundreds + **5** ten + 7 ones =	**3**	5	**7**	**357**
6 hundreds + 2 ten + **8** ones =	**6**	**2**	8	**628**

170 — Add Attack: 3 Digits

Directions: Study the examples. Follow the steps to add.

Example:

Step 1: Add the ones. Do you regroup? Yes

Step 2: Add the tens. Do you regroup? No

Step 3: Add the hundreds.

hundreds	tens	ones
	1	
3	4	8
+4	4	4
		2

hundreds	tens	ones
	1	
3	4	8
+4	4	4
	9	2

hundreds	tens	ones
	1	
3	4	8
+4	4	4
7	9	2

hundreds	tens	ones
	1	
2	1	4
+2	3	8
4	5	2

hundreds	tens	ones
	1	
3	6	8
+2	1	3
5	8	1

hundreds	tens	ones
	1	
1	1	9
+5	6	5
6	8	4

```
 418    471    334    659    736
+323   +319   +528   +127   +145
 741    790    862    786    881
```

171 — Add Attack: 3 Digits

Directions: Study the example. Follow the steps to add. Regroup when needed.

Step 1: Add the ones.
Step 2: Add the tens.
Step 3: Add the hundreds.

10 = 1 ten + 0 ones

hundreds	tens	ones
1	1	
3	4	8
+4	5	4
8	0	2

```
 348    172    575    623    369
+214   +418   +329   +268   +533
 562    590    904    891    902
```

```
 411    423    639    624    272
+299   +169   +177   +368   +469
 710    592    816    992    741
```

172 — Take It Away: 3 Digits

Directions: Study the example. Follow the steps to subtract.

Step 1: Regroup ones.
Step 2: Subtract ones.
Step 3: Subtract tens.
Step 4: Subtract hundreds.

Example:

hundreds	tens	ones
	5	12
4	6	2
−2	5	3
2	0	9

Directions: Draw a line to the correct answer. Color the kites.

347	144	963	762	287
−218	−135	−748	−553	−179

215 209 129 108 9

173 — Take It Away: 3 Digits

Directions: Subtract. Circle the **7**'s that appear in the **tens place**.

score 257

492	184
−221	−129
271	55

358	765	584	693	921
−238	−326	−435	−314	−362
120	439	149	379	559

128	744	835	248	635
−109	−674	−217	−199	−428
19	70	618	49	207

174 — All in Place

Directions: Study the example. Write the missing numbers.

Example:

1,000 100 10 1
1,000 10 1
10

2 thousands + 1 hundred + **3** tens + 2 ones = **2,132**

5,286 = **5** thousands + **2** hundreds + **8** tens + **6** ones
1,831 = **1** thousands + **8** hundreds + **3** tens + **1** ones
8,972 = **8** thousands + **9** hundreds + **7** tens + **2** ones
4,528 = **4** thousands + **5** hundreds + **2** tens + **8** ones
3,177 = **3** thousands + **1** hundreds + **7** tens + **7** ones

Directions: Draw a line to the number that has:

8 hundreds ——— 7,102
5 ones ——— 2,862
9 tens ——— 5,996
7 thousands ——— 1,485

175 — Fan-tastic!

Directions: Use the code to color the fan.

If the answer has:

9 thousands, color it **pink**.
6 thousands, color it **green**.
5 hundreds, color it orange.
8 tens, color it **red**.
3 ones, color it **blue**.

9,772   597   6,370
6,600   6,421   9,359   9,727
542
9,416

176 — Take a Bite

A graph is a drawing that shows information about numbers.

Directions: Count the apples in each row. Color the boxes to show how many apples have bites taken out of them.

Example:

1 2 3 4 5 6 7 8

177 — Something's Fishy!

Directions: Count the fish. Color the bowls to make a graph that shows the number of fish.

1 2 3 4 5 6 7 8

Directions: Use your fishbowl graphs to find the answers to the following questions. Draw a line to the correct bowl.

The most fish

The fewest fish

178 — Bunches of Bugs

Multiplication is a short way to find the sum of adding the same number a certain amount of times. For example, **4 x 7 = 28** instead of **7 + 7 + 7 + 7 = 28**.

Directions: Study the example. Solve the problems.

Example:

3 + 3 + 3 = 9
3 threes = 9
3 x 3 = 9

7 + 7 = **14**
2 sevens = **14**
2 x 7 = **14**

4 + 4 + 4 + 4 = **16**
4 fours = **16**
4 x **4** = **16**

5 + 5 = **10**
2 fives = **10**
2 x **5** = **10**

2 + 2 + 2 + 2 = **8**
4 twos = **8**
4 x **2** = **8**

179 — Good Times!

Directions: Study the example. Draw the groups and write the total.

Example:

3 x 2
2 + 2 + 2 = 6

3 x 4
4 + **4** + **4** = **12**

2 x 5
5 + **5** = **10**

5 x 3
3 + **3** + **3** + **3** + **3** = **15**

180 — Focus on Fractions

A fraction is a number that names part of a whole, such as $\frac{1}{2}$ or $\frac{1}{3}$.

Directions: Study the examples. Color the correct fraction of each shape.

Examples:

shaded part 1
equal parts 2
$\frac{1}{2}$ (one-half) shaded

shaded part 1
equal parts 3
$\frac{1}{3}$ (one-third) shaded

shaded part 1
equal parts 4
$\frac{1}{4}$ (one-fourth) shaded

Color: $\frac{1}{3}$ **red**

Color: $\frac{1}{4}$ **blue**

Color: $\frac{1}{2}$ **orange**

181 — Made in the Shade

Directions: Study the examples. Circle the fraction that shows the shaded part. Then, circle the fraction that shows the white part.

Examples:

shaded: $\frac{1}{4}$ $\frac{1}{3}$ $\boxed{\frac{1}{2}}$ white: $\frac{1}{3}$ $\boxed{\frac{1}{2}}$ $\frac{1}{4}$

shaded: $\frac{1}{4}$ $\frac{1}{2}$ $\boxed{\frac{3}{4}}$ white: $\boxed{\frac{1}{4}}$ $\frac{2}{3}$ $\frac{1}{2}$

shaded: $\frac{1}{4}$ $\boxed{\frac{1}{3}}$ $\frac{1}{2}$ white: $\frac{2}{4}$ $\boxed{\frac{2}{3}}$ $\frac{2}{2}$

shaded: $\boxed{\frac{3}{4}}$ $\frac{1}{3}$ $\frac{3}{2}$ white: $\frac{1}{2}$ $\boxed{\frac{1}{4}}$ $\frac{1}{3}$

shaded: $\frac{2}{3}$ $\boxed{\frac{2}{4}}$ $\frac{2}{2}$ white: $\frac{1}{3}$ $\boxed{\frac{2}{4}}$ $\frac{2}{2}$

shaded: $\frac{2}{4}$ $\boxed{\frac{2}{3}}$ $\frac{2}{2}$ white: $\frac{1}{2}$ $\frac{1}{4}$ $\boxed{\frac{1}{3}}$

182 — Get in Shape!

Geometry is mathematics that has to do with lines and shapes.

Directions: Color the shapes.

Color the triangles **blue**.
Color the circles **red**.
Color the squares **green**.
Color the rectangles **pink**.

183 — Tangram Tango

Directions: Cut out the tangram below. Mix up the pieces. Try to put it back together into a square.

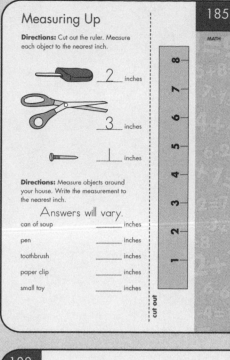

Measuring Up — 185

Directions: Cut out the ruler. Measure each object to the nearest inch.

- 2 inches
- 3 inches
- 1 inches

Directions: Measure objects around your house. Write the measurement to the nearest inch.

Answers will vary.

- can of soup ___ inches
- pen ___ inches
- toothbrush ___ inches
- paper clip ___ inches
- small toy ___ inches

Catch of the Day — 187

Directions: Use the ruler to measure the fish to the nearest inch.

- about 4 inches
- about 1 inches
- about 2 inches
- about 1 inches
- about 3 inches
- about 3 inches

Centimeter Sense — 188

A centimeter is a unit of length in the metric system. There are 2.54 centimeters in an inch.

Directions: Use a centimeter ruler to measure the crayons to the nearest centimeter.

Example: The first crayon is about 7 centimeters long.

- about 7 centimeters
- about 6 centimeters
- about 1 centimeters
- about 4 centimeters
- about 2 centimeters
- about 5 centimeters

Hour by Hour — 189

An hour is sixty minutes. The short hand of a clock tells the hour. It is written **0:00**, such as **5:00**. A half-hour is thirty minutes. When the long hand of the clock is pointing to the six, the time is on the half-hour. It is written **:30**, such as **5:30**.

Directions: Study the examples. Tell what time is on each clock.

Examples:

The minute hand is on the 12. The hour hand is on the 9. It is 9 o'clock.
9:00

The minute hand is on the 6. The hour hand is between the 4 and 5. It is 4:30.
4:30

- 2:00
- 3:30
- 1:00
- 5:30
- 10:30
- 12:00
- 9:30
- 2:30

Time's Up! — 190

The minute hand of a clock takes 5 minutes to move from one number to the next. Start at the 12 and count by fives to tell how many minutes it is past the hour.

Directions: Study the examples. Tell what time is on each clock.

Examples: 9:10   8:25

- 7:05
- 3:50
- 2:15
- 6:20
- 5:55
- 5:30
- 11:45
- 12:35
- 2:40

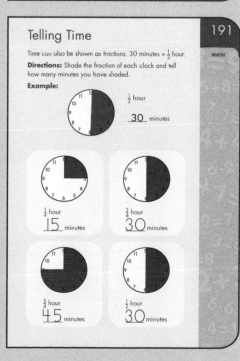

Telling Time — 191

Time can also be shown as fractions. 30 minutes = $\frac{1}{2}$ hour.

Directions: Shade the fraction of each clock and tell how many minutes you have shaded.

Example: $\frac{1}{2}$ hour — 30 minutes

- $\frac{1}{4}$ hour — 15 minutes
- $\frac{2}{4}$ hour — 30 minutes
- $\frac{3}{4}$ hour — 45 minutes
- $\frac{1}{2}$ hour — 30 minutes

192

Review

Counting

Directions: Write the number that is:

next
68, 69, _70_

one less
_56_, 57

786, 787, _788_

_649_, 650

one greater
12, _13_

843, _844_

Place Value: Tens & Ones

Directions: Draw a line to the correct number.

4 tens + 7 ones — 20
2 tens + 0 ones — 51
7 tens + 3 ones — 47
5 tens + 1 one — 73

Addition and Subtraction

Directions: Add or Subtract.

15	14	7	8	10
+5	−4	+3	−6	+7
20	10	10	2	17

193

Review

2-Digit Addition and Subtraction

Directions: Add or subtract using regrouping, if needed.

66	38	87	52	40
−37	+18	−69	−15	+17
29	56	18	37	57

84	65	99	61	56
+17	+14	−48	−36	+46
101	79	51	25	102

Place Value: Hundreds and Thousands

Directions: Draw a line to the correct number.

4 hundreds + 3 tens + 2 ones — 7,201
6 hundreds + 7 tens + 6 ones — 290
5 thousands + 3 hundreds + 7 tens + 2 ones — 432
2 hundreds + 9 tens + 0 ones — 676
7 thousands + 2 hundreds + 0 tens + 1 one — 5,372

3-Digit Addition and Subtraction

Directions: Add or subtract, remembering to regroup, if needed.

458	793	822	528	697
−248	−414	−460	+319	+108
210	379	362	847	805

194

Review

Multiplication

Directions: Solve the problems. Draw groups if necessary.

2	6	3	8	5
x8	x4	x2	x4	x3
16	24	6	32	15

Fractions

Directions: Circle the correct fraction of each shape's white part.

(1/2) 1/3 1/4   1/4 (1/3) 1/2   2/3 (2/4) 1/3   (1/4) 1/2 3/4

Graphs

Directions: Count the flowers. Color the pots to make a graph that shows the number of flowers.

1 2 3 4 5 6 7 8

195

Review

Geometry

Directions: Match the shapes.

rectangle
square
circle
triangle

Measurement

Directions: Look at the ruler. Measure the objects to the nearest inch.

1 2 3 4 5

_2_ inches
_5_ inches
CRAYON _3_ inches

Time

Directions: Tell what time is on each clock.

3:00   9:30   11:35   2:15

196

It All Makes Cents

Directions: Count the coins and write the amount.

Penny 1¢   Nickel 5¢   Dime 10¢

_16_ ¢

_27_ ¢

_26_ ¢

_38_ ¢

_21_ ¢

197

Time for a Change

Directions: Draw a line from the toy to the amount of money it costs.

198 — Counting Coins

A quarter is worth **25¢**.

Directions: Count the coins and write the amounts.

- 25 ¢
- 30 ¢
- 10 ¢
- 25 ¢
- 30 ¢
- 25 ¢
- 28 ¢
- 36 ¢

199 — Get to the Point!

A decimal is a number with one or more places to the right of a decimal point, such as 6.5 or 2.25. Money amounts are written with two places to the right of the decimal point.

25¢	10¢	5¢	1¢
$.25	$.10	$.05	$.01

Directions: Count the coins and circle the amount shown.

Example:

- (**$.17**) 23¢ $.07
- $.50 (**51¢**) 61¢
- $.28 (**36¢**) 42¢
- 37¢ 43¢ (**$.47**)

200 — Dollar Days

One dollar equals 100 cents. It is written $1.00.

Directions: Count the money and write the amounts.

- $ 1.00
- $ .36
- $ .71
- $ .29
- $ 1.25
- $ 1.00
- $ 1.55
- $ 1.21

201 — Add It Up

Directions: Write the amount of money using decimals. Then, add to find the total amount.

Example:

$$\begin{array}{r} \$1.00 \\ .05 \\ +\ .02 \\ \hline 1.07 \end{array}$$

$$\begin{array}{r} \$3.00 \\ \$\ .50 \\ \$\ .20 \\ +\$\ .01 \\ \hline 3.71 \end{array} \qquad \begin{array}{r} \$1.00 \\ \$\ .75 \\ \$\ .20 \\ +\$\ .05 \\ \hline 2.00 \end{array}$$

$$\begin{array}{r} \$2.00 \\ \$\ .25 \\ +\$\ .40 \\ \hline 2.65 \end{array} \qquad \begin{array}{r} \$1.00 \\ \$\ .25 \\ \$\ .30 \\ +\$\ .15 \\ \hline 1.70 \end{array}$$

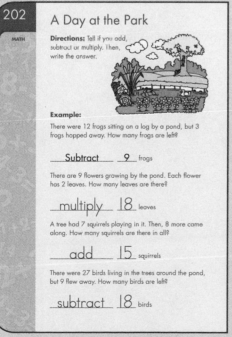

202 — A Day at the Park

Directions: Tell if you add, subtract or multiply. Then, write the answer.

Example:

There were 12 frogs sitting on a log by a pond, but 3 frogs hopped away. How many frogs are left?

__Subtract__ __9__ frogs

There are 9 flowers growing by the pond. Each flower has 2 leaves. How many leaves are there?

__multiply__ __18__ leaves

A tree had 7 squirrels playing in it. Then, 8 more came along. How many squirrels are there in all?

__add__ __15__ squirrels

There were 27 birds living in the trees around the pond, but 9 flew away. How many birds are left?

__subtract__ __18__ birds

203 — Time to Solve It

Directions: Solve each problem.

Tracy wakes up at 7:00. She has 30 minutes before her bus comes. What time does her bus come?

__7:30__

Vera walks her dog for 15 minutes after supper. She finishes supper at 6:30. When does she get home from walking her dog?

__6:45__

Chip practices the piano for 30 minutes when he gets home from school. He gets home at 3:30. When does he stop practicing?

__4:00__

Tanya starts mowing the grass at 4:30. She finishes at 5:00. For how many minutes does she mow the lawn?

__30__ minutes

204

MATH

Toy Time

Directions: Read each problem. Use the pictures to help you solve the problems.

Ben bought a ball. He had 11¢ left. How much money did he have at the start? 40 ¢

Tara has 75¢. She buys a car. How much money does she have left? 30 ¢

Leah wants to buy a doll and a ball. She has 80¢. How much more money does she need? 8 ¢

Jacob has 95¢. He buys the car and the ball. How much more money does he need to buy a doll for his sister? 38 ¢

Kim paid three quarters, one dime and three pennies for a hat. How much did it cost? 88 ¢